The New Joys of Jell-O®
BRAND GELATIN
recipe book

How to Use
The New Joys of Jell-O®
BRAND GELATIN
recipe book

The joys of Jell-O Gelatin are never ending. The same Jell-O Gelatin that made a cool dessert many years ago is still a shimmering example of versatility. Make it simple or elegant. Make it dessert or salad. Make it for family or for special occasion. In any form, Jell-O Gelatin has a light, refreshing, fresh fruity taste.

If you're new or a pro to the world of Jell-O Gelatin, you'll love THE NEW JOYS OF JELL-O Recipe Book. Start at the beginning of this book with the very fast and easy-to-make recipes and work your way to the more intricate recipes. The chapter, "Basic Preparation Hints," is divided into three sections—definitions, techniques, and tips—to help you make the recipes in this book in the best way possible. Throughout the book you'll find helpful hints—little suggestions to help you make even the simplest recipe turn out perfectly professional. You can use the wide space in the margins to jot down your own timesaving tips for each recipe.

Make this the beginning of a rewarding experience for you and your family. Just start with Jell-O Gelatin.

For additional copies of
The New Joys of Jell-O Recipe Book
Send $1.00 (no stamps) for each copy desired along with your name, address and ZIP Code to: The New Joys of Jell-O
Box 3070, Kankakee, Illinois 60901.

TABLE OF CONTENTS

Nice Easy Things to Do With Jell-O® BRAND GELATIN Page 4

Start with Jell-O® BRAND GELATIN Page 6

Family Desserts Page 20

Bring on the Super Desserts Page 32

Centerpiece Desserts Page 44

Salads that Help Make the Meal Page 64

Sociable Side Salads Page 76

Salads for the Slim Life Page 84

Salads for Special Events Page 92

Especially for Junior Cooks Page 100

Things You Never Thought Of Page 108

Basic Preparation Hints Page 116

Serve it in Style Page 124

Index Page 126

Cover Desserts Page 126

Nice Easy Things to Do With Jell-O®

BRAND GELATIN

Start with a package of Jell-O Gelatin. Then work *simple* wonders. These recipes are fast and easy to make, with plenty of how-to tips to guide you along the way.

Learn the easiest and best way to work imaginatively with Jell-O Gelatin. Cube it, flake it, whip it, blend it, cream it, layer it, mold it, or unmold it. With a few simple hints, you can easily and quickly create such super specialties as Melon Cooler or Double Strawberry Dessert.

Jell-O Gelatin also makes the most of familiar ingredients. All the things you need can come right from your own kitchen shelf or refrigerator. Make it simply splendid—all with a few nice, easy things to do with Jell-O Gelatin.

Start with Jell-O®

BRAND GELATIN

Then improvise with the ordinary. Amazing, the way Jell-O Gelatin pulls simple ingredients together into a sparkling salad or dessert. And for those simple ingredients you can use what you have on hand in your own kitchen. Such packaged, canned, or frozen foods can be used with Jell-O Gelatin in easy, quick dishes. All of these ingredients can be put to good use with the recipes in this book—or create your own special flavors, textures, colors, and forms with ingredients from your own kitchen.

FROM THE KITCHEN SHELF

Whipped topping mix
Flaked coconut
Canned fruits and vegetables
Candied fruits
Honey
Canned cranberry sauce
Miniature marshmallows
Canned vegetable juices
Carbonated beverages
Instant coffee
Pudding and pie filling mixes
Graham crackers or graham cracker crumbs
Pickles
Nuts
Fruit preserves and jellies
Flavoring extracts—especially vanilla,
    almond, and peppermint
Wines—especially port, sherry, rosé,
    white wine, and sauterne
Liqueurs
Canned tuna, crabmeat, salmon, and chicken
Olives—ripe, green, and stuffed
Pimientos
Mayonnaise
Candied ginger

FROM THE FREEZER

Frozen pie and tart shells
Frozen fruits and vegetables
Frozen fruit juices
Frozen whipped topping
Ice creams and sherbets

FROM THE REFRIGERATOR

Cream
Yogurt
Cream cheese
Fresh fruits and vegetables
Leftover meats and poultry

QUICK FRUIT DESSERT

    1 package (3 oz.) Jell-O Gelatin,
          any flavor
  1½ cups boiling water
    1 package (10 oz.) Birds Eye Quick
          Thaw Fruits, any variety

Dissolve gelatin in boiling water. Add frozen fruit; stir gently until fruit thaws and separates. (In some cases, gelatin will begin to thicken.) Chill. In about 30 minutes, gelatin will be soft set and ready to eat. In about 1 hour, gelatin will be set, but not firm. Makes about 3 cups or about 6 servings.

Note: Setting times will vary depending upon the temperature of the frozen fruit and the size of the pieces of fruit.

MELON COOLER

    1 can (12 fl. oz.) citrus based
          carbonated beverage
    1 package (3 oz.) Jell-O Orange Gelatin
  1½ cups diced watermelon, cantaloupe
          or honeydew melon

Bring 1 cup carbonated beverage to a boil. Add to gelatin and stir until dissolved. Add water to remaining carbonated beverage to make ¾ cup liquid; stir into gelatin mixture. Chill until thickened; then fold in diced melon. Pour into 4-cup mold and chill until firm—about 4 hours. Unmold. Garnish with prepared Dream Whip Whipped Topping and mint leaves, if desired. Makes 3 cups or 6 servings.

Add zip to Jell-O Gelatin by substituting a carbonated soft drink for part or all of the water. Use cola, ginger ale, root beer, or any of the carbonated lemon and lime flavored mixers.

PEACH BAVARIAN

1 can (29 oz.) sliced peaches
1 package (3 oz.) Jell-O Lemon Gelatin
¼ cup sugar
Dash of salt
1 cup boiling water
¼ teaspoon almond extract
2 cups (or one 4½-oz. container)
    Birds Eye Cool Whip Non-Dairy
    Whipped Topping, thawed

When a recipe specifies a certain amount of fresh or canned fruit, be sure to drain the fruit thoroughly before measuring. The fruit juice or syrup can then be used as part of the liquid specified in the recipe.

Drain peaches, reserving ⅓ cup of the syrup. Chop peaches. Dissolve gelatin, sugar, and salt in boiling water. Add reserved syrup. Chill until slightly thickened. Blend almond extract into whipped topping; gradually blend into gelatin, then fold in the peaches. Pour into 5-cup mold. Chill until firm—about 4 hours. Unmold. Makes 5 cups or 10 servings.

MINTED PINEAPPLE RELISH

1 package (3 oz.) Jell-O Lime Gelatin
Dash of salt
¾ cup boiling water
1 can (13½ oz.) crushed pineapple
4 drops mint or peppermint extract
2½ teaspoons vinegar

Dissolve gelatin and salt in boiling water. Stir in remaining ingredients. Chill until thickened. Pour into 3- or 4-cup mold or individual molds. Chill until firm—about 4 hours. Unmold. Makes about 2½ cups or 6 to 8 servings.

Note: Mixture may be chilled in a serving bowl; do not unmold.

CUBED GELATIN
(photographed above)

 1 package (3 oz.) Jell-O Gelatin,
    any flavor
 1 cup boiling water
 ¾ cup cold water

Dissolve gelatin in boiling water. Add cold water and pour into 8- or 9-inch square pan. Chill until firm—at least 3 hours. Then cut in cubes, using sharp knife which has been dipped in hot water. To remove cubes from pan, apply warm wet cloth over bottom of pan. When cubes are slightly loosened, remove with spatula. Or quickly dip pan in warm water and invert on wax paper. Serve in dessert dishes plain, or with fresh or drained canned fruit. Makes 4 servings.

For very firm cubes, reduce cold water to ½ cup.

For softer cubes, increase cold water to 1 cup.

GELATIN AND FRUIT
(photographed above)

Alternately layer prepared Jell-O Gelatin, any flavor, with fresh fruit in individual dishes.

DOUBLE STRAWBERRY DESSERT
(photographed above)

> 2 packages (3 oz. each) or 1 package (6 oz.) Jell-O Strawberry Gelatin
> ¼ cup jelly, any red flavor
> Dash of salt (optional)
> 3 cups boiling water
> ½ cup sour cream
> 1 package (10 oz.) Birds Eye Quick Thaw Strawberries

Dissolve gelatin, jelly, and salt in boiling water. Measure ½ cup of the mixture; blend into sour cream; chill. Add frozen strawberries to the remaining gelatin mixture and stir with a fork until berries are separated and thawed. Pour into a 4- or 5-cup serving bowl. Chill until firm— at least 3 hours. Spoon firm gelatin into individual dessert dishes. Beat sour cream mixture until smooth; spoon over dessert. Makes about 4 cups or 8 servings.

Note: Recipe may also be chilled in a 4- or 5-cup mold; chill until firm—about 4 hours. Unmold. Serve with sour cream topping.

FROSTED FRESH GRAPES

- 2 pounds seedless grapes
- 1 egg white, slightly beaten
- 1 package (3 oz.) Jell-O Gelatin, any flavor

Cut bunches of grapes into small clusters. Dip clusters, one at a time, into beaten egg white. Hold to permit excess to drain off, then sprinkle with gelatin. Chill on tray covered with wax paper for about 3 hours. Use as a garnish for salad or dessert, or serve as a dessert. Frosted grapes may be stored in refrigerator overnight.

JELLIED GINGER-UPPER

- 1 package (3 oz.) Jell-O Gelatin, any red flavor
- 1 cup boiling water
- 1 bottle (7 fl. oz.) ginger ale
- 1½ teaspoons lemon juice
- 1 cup diced fresh or drained canned pears or peaches

To add fruits and vegetables, chill the gelatin until it is thickened (spoon drawn through gelatin leaves a definite impression) before adding other ingredients. If gelatin isn't thick enough, fruits and vegetables may float or sink.

Dissolve gelatin in boiling water. Gradually add ginger ale and lemon juice. Chill until thickened; stir in pears. Spoon into individual molds or a 3-cup mold. Chill until firm. Unmold and garnish with Frosted Fresh Grapes and green leaves, if desired. Makes about 3 cups or 6 servings.

BLACK RASPBERRY ICE CREAM DESSERT

1 package (3 oz.) Jell-O Black
    Raspberry Gelatin
1 cup boiling water
¾ cup cold water*
¼ cup sherry wine*
1 pint vanilla ice cream

*Or increase cold water to 1 cup and omit the wine.

Dissolve gelatin in boiling water. Add cold water and wine. Add ice cream, by spoonfuls, stirring until melted. Chill until slightly thickened; then stir, and spoon into dessert dishes. Chill—about 1 hour. Makes 3½ cups or 7 servings.

ORANGE SNOW

1 package (3 oz.) Jell-O Orange-
    Pineapple or Orange Gelatin
⅛ teaspoon salt
1 cup boiling water
¾ cup orange juice
½ teaspoon grated orange rind
1 egg white

You can also transform Jell-O Gelatin into a frothy dessert without adding any extra ingredients. Prepare Jell-O Gelatin as directed, chilling until very thick. Beat with rotary beater or electric mixer until fluffy and thick—about double in volume. Chill until firm. Looks especially attractive when served in individual glasses or in a pretty glass serving dish.

Dissolve gelatin and salt in boiling water in a bowl. Add orange juice and rind. Place bowl of gelatin in larger bowl of ice and water, stir until slightly thickened. Add egg white; whip with rotary beater or electric mixer until fluffy, thick, and about double in volume. Pile lightly in dessert glasses or pour into an 8-inch square pan. Chill until firm—about 3 hours. If pan is used, cut into rectangles before serving. Serve with Birds Eye Quick Thaw Strawberries or sweetened sliced fresh strawberries, if desired. Makes 5 cups or 6 servings.

CHIFFON MARBLE
(photographed above)

- 1 package (3 oz.) Jell-O Lime Gelatin
- ¾ cup boiling water
- 2 cups ice cubes
- 1 cup Birds Eye Cool Whip Non-Dairy
  Whipped Topping, thawed*

*Or used 1 cup prepared Dream Whip
Whipped Topping.

Dissolve gelatin in boiling water. Add ice cubes
and stir constantly until gelatin starts to thicken
—2 to 3 minutes. Remove any unmelted ice.
Remove ¾ cup gelatin mixture; set aside. Fold
whipped topping into remaining gelatin. Alternately spoon plain gelatin and whipped topping
mixture into 4 dessert glasses. Carefully zigzag
spatula or knife through mixture to marble.
Chill. Makes about 2 cups or 4 servings.

An easy trick to shorten
the required chilling time
—substitute 2 cups of
ice cubes for 1 cup of
cold water when preparing
Jell-O Gelatin. Stir about
3 minutes to melt ice, or
until gelatin is thickened.
Remove any unmelted ice.

STRAWBERRY YOGURT WHIP
(photographed above)

    1 package (3 oz.) Jell-O
          Strawberry Gelatin
    1 cup boiling water
  ¾ cup cold water
    1 container (8 oz.) strawberry yogurt

Dissolve gelatin in boiling water. Add cold water. Chill until slightly thickened. Add yogurt and beat with rotary beater until mixture is light and fluffy. Pour into punch cups or individual serving dishes. Chill about 2 hours. Makes 4 cups or 8 servings.

QUICK CRÈME DE MENTHE FRAPPÉ

    1 package (3 oz.) Jell-O Lemon or
          Lime Gelatin
   ¾ cup boiling water
1 ½ cups crushed ice
    1 tablespoon crème de menthe liqueur

Combine gelatin and boiling water in blender
container. Cover and blend at low speed for 30
seconds or until the gelatin is dissolved. Add
crushed ice and crème de menthe. Blend at
high speed until the ice is melted—about 30
seconds. Pour into 4-cup ring mold. Chill at
least 30 minutes. Unmold. Or pour into individual sherbet glasses or serving bowl and chill
until soft set—5 minutes in glass and 20 minutes
in bowl. Makes 4 cups or 6 servings.

WINE GELATIN DESSERT

       1 package (3 oz.) Jell-O Gelatin, any
             red flavor
1 to 2 tablespoons sugar
       1 cup boiling water
      ¼ cup cold water
      ½ cup dry red wine or sherry

Dissolve gelatin and sugar in boiling water.
Add cold water and wine. Pour into individual
molds. Chill until firm—at least 3 hours. Unmold.
Serve with custard sauce, if desired. Makes
about 2 cups or 4 servings.

For best results, dissolve
Jell-O Gelatin *completely*
in boiling water or
other liquid. For a clear
uniformly set mold,
Jell-O Gelatin *must* be
completely dissolved.

MOLDED TOMATO RELISH

1 can (16 oz.) stewed tomatoes
1 package (3 oz.) Jell-O Lemon or
  Strawberry Gelatin
½ teaspoon salt
1 tablespoon vinegar

Empty cans make easy molds for gelatin relishes or frozen salads. After dipping can in warm water, puncture bottom of can, and unmold.

Pour tomatoes into saucepan, saving can to use as a mold. Bring tomatoes to a boil. Reduce heat and simmer 2 minutes. Add gelatin, salt, and vinegar; stir until gelatin is dissolved. Pour into can. Chill until firm—about 4 hours. Then dip can in warm water, puncture bottom of can, and unmold. Makes about 2 cups or 6 servings.

QUICK ORANGE SALAD

1 package (3 oz.) Jell-O Orange Gelatin
  Dash of salt
1 cup boiling water
2 teaspoons lemon juice
2 cups ice cubes
1 cup orange sections
½ cup halved seedless green grapes*

*Or use ½ cup finely chopped apple *or* ½ cup sliced banana.

Dissolve gelatin and salt in boiling water. Stir in lemon juice. Add ice cubes and stir constantly until gelatin starts to thicken—3 to 5 minutes. Remove any unmelted ice. Gently stir in oranges and grapes. Pour into serving bowl or individual dishes. Chill until firm— about 2 hours. Makes 3 cups or 6 servings.

Family Desserts

Jell-O Gelatin looks as cool and appetizing in everyday family desserts as it does in dazzling party creations. But the true beauty in these family desserts is the fun and ease you'll have in making and in serving them.

You can make each serving of dessert special. Set aside several servings of plain gelatin to chill for the purists in the family, then add chopped fruit or nuts to the remainder of servings. Toppings and garnishes can be added separately, too. Try an ice cream topping for your active young second baseman, or a sprinkle of chopped mint leaves for his waistline-watcher father.

Just watch those smiles when you serve such family desserts as Fruit Refresher or Double Orange Whip. Ordinary to make, yet out-of-the-ordinary to eat. Jell-O Gelatin—the uncomplicated dessert pleaser for everyone in your family.

PEACH-BANANA DESSERT
(photographed on page 20)

> 1 can (1 lb.) sliced peaches
> 1 package (3 oz.) Jell-O
>   Strawberry Gelatin
> 1 cup boiling water
> 1 banana, sliced

Drain peaches, measuring syrup. Add water to syrup to make 1 cup. Dissolve gelatin in boiling water. Add measured liquid. Pour into individual dessert dishes. Add peaches and banana. Chill until set. Makes about 4 cups or 8 servings.

FRUIT DELIGHT
(photographed on page 20)

> 1 can (8¾ oz.) fruit cocktail*
> 1 package (3 oz.) Jell-O Gelatin,
>   any flavor
> 1½ cups crushed ice

*Or use 1 can (8¾ oz.) crushed pineapple, sliced peaches, or diced pears.

Drain fruit cocktail reserving syrup. Add water to syrup to make ¾ cup; bring to a boil. Combine gelatin and boiling liquid in blender container. Cover and blend on low speed for 30 seconds or until the gelatin is dissolved. Add crushed ice; blend at high speed until the ice is melted—about 30 seconds. Pour mixture into individual serving dishes. Spoon fruit cocktail into each dish. Chill until set—about 10 minutes. Makes about 4 servings.

Do *not* add fresh or frozen pineapple, figs, mangoes, or papayas or frozen fruit juice blends containing these fruits— an enzyme in these fruits, when fresh, keeps Jell-O Gelatin from setting. When cooked or canned, these fruits are excellent in Jell-O Gelatin.

FRUIT REFRESHER
(photographed on page 20)

1½ cups fresh berries or other fruit or combination of fruits

¼ cup sugar

1 package (3 oz.) Jell-O Gelatin, any fruit flavor

1 cup boiling water

Combine fruit and sugar; let stand 10 minutes. Drain, measuring syrup. Add water to syrup to make 1½ cups. Dissolve gelatin in boiling water. Add measured liquid. Chill until thickened. Stir in fruit. Chill. Dessert will be soft-set, not firm. Spoon into individual dessert dishes, sherbet glasses, or a serving bowl. Serve plain or with cream. Makes about 4 cups or 6 to 8 servings.

GINGER PEACH DESSERT
(photographed on page 20)

1 package (3 oz.) Jell-O Orange Gelatin

1 cup boiling water

1 cup ginger ale

1 cup sweetened diced fresh peaches or diced canned peaches, drained

Dissolve gelatin in boiling water. Add ginger ale; chill until thickened. Fold in peaches; spoon into individual dishes. Chill until firm. Unmold. Makes 2¾ cups or 5 servings.

ORANGE PARFAIT
(photographed on pages 24-25)

  1 package (3 oz.) Jell-O Orange Gelatin
  1 cup boiling water
  2 cups ice cubes
  ½ cup orange sections
  ½ cup chopped apple
  ½ cup prepared Dream Whip
      Whipped Topping

Dissolve gelatin in boiling water. Add ice cubes
and stir constantly until gelatin starts to thicken
—3 to 5 minutes. Remove any unmelted ice.
Layer gelatin in parfait glasses with fruit and
whipped topping, beginning and ending with
gelatin. Chill 1 hour. Makes 4 or 5 servings.

DOUBLE ORANGE WHIP

  1 bottle (7 fl. oz.) ginger ale
  1 package (3 oz.) Jell-O Orange Gelatin
  1 cup cold orange juice

To vary the flavor of a
Jell-O Gelatin dessert,
use fruit juice for all
or part of the liquid.

Bring ginger ale to a boil. Add gelatin; stir
until dissolved. Add orange juice. Place bowl
of gelatin in larger bowl of ice and water,
stir until slightly thickened. Whip with rotary
beater or electric mixer until fluffy and thick,
and about double in volume. Spoon into
individual dessert dishes. Chill until set — at least
30 minutes. Makes 4 cups or 4 to 6 servings.

LAYERED BAVARIAN
(photographed on page 20)

    1 package (3 oz.) Jell-O Gelatin,
          any flavor
    1 cup boiling water
    ½ cup cold water
    1 cup vanilla ice cream

Place gelatin in an 8- or 9-inch square metal pan. Add boiling water and stir until gelatin is completely dissolved. Measure ½ cup into a bowl; set aside. Add cold water to remaining gelatin in the pan; freeze until thickened—about 15 minutes. Meanwhile, blend ice cream into reserved gelatin. Spoon thickened clear gelatin into dessert glasses; top with ice cream-gelatin mixture. Or spoon ice cream-gelatin into glasses, top with the clear thickened gelatin. Chill 30 minutes. Makes about 2½ cups or 4 or 5 servings.

FRUIT FLAVOR FLAKES
(photographed on page 20)

    1 package (3 oz.) Jell-O Gelatin,
          any flavor
    1 cup boiling water
    ¾ cup cold water

Dissolve gelatin in boiling water. Add cold water. Pour into a shallow pan; chill until firm. Break into small flakes with a fork, or force through potato ricer or large-meshed strainer. Pile lightly in dessert dishes. Garnish with fruit, prepared whipped topping, or whipped cream, if desired. Makes 4 servings.

JELLIED PEACH MELBA
(photographed above)

- 2 packages (3 oz. each) or 1 package (6 oz.) Jell-O Raspberry Gelatin
- 2 cups boiling water
- 1 tablespoon lemon juice
- ½ cup cold water
- 1 package (10 oz.) Birds Eye Quick Thaw Peaches, slightly thawed
- 1 package (10 oz.) Birds Eye Quick Thaw Red Raspberries, slightly thawed
- 1 pint vanilla ice cream

Dissolve gelatin in boiling water. Add lemon juice and cold water. Add frozen fruit and stir gently until fruit thaws and separates—gelatin may begin to thicken. Pour into 5-cup ring mold. Chill until firm—4 hours or overnight. Unmold. Just before serving, fill center of ring with scoops of ice cream. Or chill mixture in individual dessert dishes and top each with a scoop of ice cream. Makes 5 cups or 8 to 10 servings.

Before unmolding, make certain that Jell-O Gelatin is completely firm. It should not feel sticky on top and should not sag toward the side if mold or dish is tilted.

FROSTY MANDARIN DESSERT
(photographed above)

   1 can (11 oz.) mandarin orange sections
   2 packages (3 oz. each) or 1 package
      (6 oz.) Jell-O Orange Gelatin
   2 cups boiling water
   1 pint orange sherbet

Drain oranges, measuring syrup. Add water to syrup to make 1 cup. Dissolve gelatin in boiling water. Add measured liquid. Add sherbet by spoonfuls, stirring until melted. Chill until thickened.

Fold in oranges, reserving a few for garnish. Pour into a serving bowl or individual serving dishes. Chill until set—at least one hour. Garnish with reserved mandarin orange sections and mint leaves, if desired. Makes about 5 cups or 8 servings.

PASTEL DESSERT

    1 package (3¼ oz.) Jell-O Vanilla
        Pudding and Pie Filling
    1 package (3 oz.) Jell-O Gelatin,
        any flavor
 2½ cups water
    1 envelope Dream Whip Whipped
        Topping Mix

Combine pudding mix, gelatin, and water in a
saucepan. Cook and stir over medium heat
until mixture comes to a *full* boil and is
thickened and clear. Remove from heat. Chill
until slightly thickened.

Prepare whipped topping mix as directed on
package. Thoroughly blend into the chilled
pudding mixture. Spoon into individual sherbet
glasses or serving bowl. Chill until firm—
about 3 hours. Makes about 4 cups or 6 to 8
servings.

JELLIED PRUNE WHIP

    1 package (3 oz.) Jell-O Orange or
        Lemon Gelatin
    1 cup boiling water
  ¾ cup cold water
  ¼ teaspoon salt
  ¼ teaspoon grated orange rind
  ¼ cup sugar
 1½ cups chopped cooked prune pulp
        (about 1 lb. dried prunes)

Dissolve gelatin in boiling water. Add cold
water, salt, and orange rind. Place bowl
of gelatin in a larger bowl of ice and water.
Stir until slightly thickened; then whip until
fluffy and thick. Add sugar to prune pulp
and fold into whipped gelatin. Pile lightly in
sherbet glasses. Chill until set—at least 1 hour.
Serve with custard sauce or light cream.
Makes 5 cups or 8 to 10 servings.

FRESH STRAWBERRY PIE

  1 package (3 oz.) Jell-O Strawberry or
     Strawberry-Banana Gelatin
1⅔ cups boiling water
  2 tablespoons sugar
  2 cups (or one 4½-oz. container)
     Birds Eye Cool Whip Non-Dairy
     Whipped Topping, thawed
     Red food coloring
  1 baked 9-inch crumb crust or pie
     shell, cooled
1½ cups fresh strawberry halves

Dissolve gelatin in boiling water. Remove
½ cup and chill until slightly thickened. Fold
the slightly thickened gelatin and sugar
into the whipped topping. Add a few drops
of food coloring. Chill again, if necessary, until
mixture will mound. Line bottom and sides of
crumb crust with the whipped topping mixture,
mounding high around edge. Chill. Meanwhile,
chill remaining gelatin until thickened. Stir in
strawberries. Spoon into the center of the
whipped topping-lined crust without covering
the high rim around the edge. Chill until firm—
at least 3 hours.

Bring on the Super Desserts

"I'll bring the dessert."

Ah, what musical words to the ears of any busy hostess. Super Desserts are Jell-O Gelatin desserts with a certain special look that can make a party out of a family dinner, or turn a casual get-together with neighbors into a memorable evening.

Despite their party flair, these are all easily-made desserts. With a fast blender method or an ice cube method for quick preparation, you can create the spectacular.

These Super Desserts, such as the Strawberries Romanoff on the opposite page, are also for toting to buffet parties, showers, church dinners, or Thanksgiving at your in-laws.

So bring on the Super Desserts. Just be prepared to share your recipe before the evening is over!

STRAWBERRIES ROMANOFF
(photographed on page 32)

>   1 pint strawberries, washed
>   and stemmed
>   2 tablespoons sugar
>   2 packages (3 oz. each) or 1 package
>   (6 oz.) Jell-O Strawberry Gelatin
>   2 cups boiling water
>   2 tablespoons brandy*
>   1 tablespoon Cointreau or
>   Curacao liqueur*
>   2 cups (or one 4½-oz. container)
>   Birds Eye Cool Whip Non-Dairy
>   Whipped Topping, thawed**

*Or use ½ teaspoon brandy extract and 3
tablespoons orange juice.

**Or use 1 envelope Dream Whip Whipped
Topping Mix prepared as directed
on package.

Set aside a few whole berries for garnish, if
desired. Slice remaining berries, add sugar,
and let stand 15 minutes. Drain berries,
measuring syrup. Add water to syrup to make
1 cup. Dissolve gelatin in boiling water.
Measure ¾ cup of the gelatin; add brandy,
liqueur, and ½ cup of the measured liquid.
Chill until slightly thickened. Fold in whipped
topping. Pour into 5- or 6-cup mold. Chill until
set, but not firm.

Add remaining ½ cup measured liquid to
remaining gelatin. Chill until thickened. Stir in
strawberries. Spoon into mold. Chill until
firm—about 4 hours, or overnight. Unmold,
garnish with berries. Makes 6 cups or 8 to
10 servings.

Note: Recipe may be doubled; chill in 12 cup
glass salad or punch bowl (as shown on
page 32). Do not unmold. Garnish with mint
sprigs.

TOPAZ PARFAIT
(photographed on page 41)

1 cup strong coffee
1 package (3 oz.) Jell-O Lemon Gelatin
⅓ cup sugar
½ cup cold water*
¼ cup brandy or dark rum*
1 envelope Dream Whip Whipped
   Topping Mix
2 tablespoons brown sugar
1 tablespoon brandy or dark rum**

*Or increase cold water to ¾ cup and add
1 teaspoon brandy extract.
**Or use ½ teaspoon brandy extract.

To double a recipe, use two 3-oz. packages or one 6-oz. package of Jell-O Gelatin and twice the amounts of the other ingredients except salt, vinegar, and lemon juice —you'll find about 1½ times the amounts of these ingredients are sufficient.

Bring coffee to a boil. Add gelatin and sugar and stir until dissolved. Add cold water and ¼ cup brandy. Pour into an 8-inch square pan. Chill until firm—about 4 hours. Cut into cubes. Prepare whipped topping as directed adding brown sugar and 1 tablespoon brandy. Layer coffee cubes and topping in parfait glasses or top cubes in sherbet glasses with topping. Makes 4 servings.

Note: Recipe may be doubled.

CHERRY BURGUNDY DESSERT

1 package (3 oz.) Jell-O Cherry Gelatin
1 cup boiling water
½ cup Burgundy or Port Wine
¼ cup cold water
1 can (8¾ oz.) sliced peaches, drained
   Dash of cinnamon
1 cup prepared Dream Whip
   Whipped Topping

Dissolve gelatin in boiling water. Add wine and cold water. Chill until slightly thickened. Stir in peaches. Pour into 3-cup mold or individual molds. Chill until firm—at least 4 hours. Stir cinnamon into prepared whipped topping. Unmold gelatin; garnish with additional sliced peaches and spiced whipped topping, if desired. Makes 2¼ cups or 4 servings.

PORTED CHERRY DESSERT
(photographed above)

    1 package (10 oz.) Birds Eye Quick Thaw
          Sweet Cherries, thawed
    1 tablespoon lemon juice
  ½ cup (about) port wine
    1 package (3 oz.) Jell-O Cherry Gelatin
1½ cups crushed ice
  ½ cup (about) sour cream

Drain cherries, measuring syrup. Reserve 6
cherries for garnish. Add lemon juice to syrup;
add wine to make 1 cup, and bring to a boil.
Combine gelatin and boiling liquid in blender
container. Cover and blend at low speed
for 30 seconds or until gelatin is dissolved. Add
crushed ice and blend at high speed until ice
is melted—about 30 seconds. Pour into
individual dishes or wine glasses. Add cherries.
Garnish with sour cream and reserved cherries.
Chill. Makes about 4 cups or 6 to 8 servings.

MELON BUBBLE
(photographed above)

- 1 package (3 oz.) Jell-O Lemon Gelatin
- 1 cup boiling water
- ¾ cup cold water
- ¼ cup Cointreau liqueur or orange juice*
- 1 cup melon balls

*Or omit liqueur or juice; increase cold water to 1 cup.

Dissolve gelatin in boiling water. Add cold water and liqueur. Chill 1⅓ cups until thickened. Fold in melon balls. Pour into serving bowl and chill until set, but not firm. Set bowl with remaining gelatin in a larger bowl of ice and water. Stir until slightly thickened then whip until fluffy and thick, and about double in volume. Pour over set gelatin. Chill until firm —about 3 hours. Garnish with additional melon balls and mint leaves, if desired. Makes 3½ cups or 6 servings.

Note: Recipe may be chilled in individual dessert dishes.

LEMON CHIFFON PIE

  3 egg yolks, slightly beaten
  1 cup water
  ¼ cup sugar
  1 package (3 oz.) Jell-O Lemon Gelatin
  ½ cup water
  3 tablespoons lemon juice
  1½ teaspoons grated lemon rind
  3 egg whites
    Dash of salt
  ¼ cup sugar
  1 baked 9-inch pie shell or
    crumb crust, cooled

Combine egg yolks and 1 cup water in sauce-pan; add ¼ cup sugar. Cook and stir over low heat until mixture is slightly thickened and just comes to a boil. Remove from heat. Add gelatin and stir until dissolved. Add ½ cup water, the lemon juice, and rind. Chill until slightly thickened. Beat egg whites and salt until foamy. Gradually beat in ¼ cup sugar and continue beating until mixture will stand in stiff peaks. Fold in thickened gelatin; blend well. Chill again, if necessary, until mixture will mound. Spoon into pie shell. Chill until firm —about 4 hours.

ORANGE CHIFFON PIE

Prepare Lemon Chiffon Pie as directed, substi-tuting orange flavor gelatin, orange juice, and orange rind for the lemon flavor gelatin, lemon juice, and lemon rind.

CHERRY CHIFFON
(photographed on page 41)

    1 package (3 oz.) Jell-O Cherry Gelatin
    ¾ cup boiling water
    1 cup ice cubes
    1 can (8¾ oz.) pitted sweet dark
         cherries, drained
    1 package (3 oz.) Jell-O Cherry Gelatin
    ¾ cup boiling water
    1 cup ice cubes
    2 cups (or one 4½-oz. container)
         Birds Eye Cool Whip Non-Dairy
         Whipped Topping, thawed*

*Or use 2 cups prepared Dream Whip
Whipped Topping.

Dissolve 1 package gelatin in ¾ cup boiling
water. Add 1 cup ice cubes and stir about
3 minutes, until gelatin is slightly thickened.
Remove any unmelted ice. Stir in fruit. Pour into
a 5-cup mold. Place in refrigerator. Dissolve
second package of gelatin in ¾ cup boiling
water. Add ice cubes and stir about 3 minutes,
until gelatin is slightly thickened. Remove any
unmelted ice. Fold in whipped topping. Pour
into mold over fruited layer. Refrigerate at least
1 hour. Makes about 5 cups or 10 servings.

STRAWBERRY CHIFFON

Prepare Cherry Chiffon as directed, substituting
strawberry flavor gelatin and 1 cup sliced
fresh strawberries for the cherry flavor gelatin
and the cherries.

JELLIED HOLIDAY NOG
(photographed on page 40)

- 2 packages (3 oz. each) or 1 package (6 oz.) Jell-O Lemon Gelatin
- 2 packages (3¼ oz. each) Jell-O Vanilla Pudding and Pie Filling
- 2 tablespoons sugar
- 5 cups water

- 2 envelopes Dream Whip Whipped Topping Mix
- 1 teaspoon rum extract
- 1 teaspoon vanilla
- ½ teaspoon nutmeg

If capacity of a bowl is unknown, fill it with water; then measure the water and use a 3-oz. package of Jell-O Gelatin for each 2 cups of liquid required to fill the bowl.

Combine gelatin, pudding mix, and sugar in a large saucepan. Add water. Cook and stir over medium heat until mixture comes to a *full* boil. Remove from heat. Chill until thickened.

Prepare whipped topping mix as directed on package. Thoroughly blend prepared whipped topping, rum extract, vanilla, and nutmeg into the thickened pudding mixture. Pour into a large serving bowl or punch bowl. Chill until firm—at least 4 hours or overnight. Garnish with cherries and mint leaves, and serve with Cranberry Orange Sauce, if desired. Makes about 8 cups or 16 servings.

CRANBERRY ORANGE SAUCE

- 2 cups fresh cranberries
- 1 medium orange
- 2 cups sugar
- 2 tablespoons Minute Tapioca
- 1 cup water
- 1 tablespoon Cointreau liqueur

Grind cranberries and orange (skin and pulp) and set aside. Combine sugar, tapioca, and water in a saucepan; let stand 5 minutes. Cook and stir over medium heat until mixture comes to a boil; reduce heat and simmer 3 minutes. Add ground cranberries and orange and simmer 3 minutes longer. Cool 20 minutes. Just before serving, add liqueur. Serve with Molded Holiday Nog. Makes about 3½ cups.

PINK LADY PIE

(photographed on page 41)

3 egg yolks, slightly beaten
1 cup water
¼ cup sugar
1 package (3 oz.) Jell-O Gelatin,
    any red flavor
½ cup cold water
1 tablespoon lemon juice
1 tablespoon grenadine syrup (optional)
1 envelope Dream Whip Whipped
    Topping Mix
3 egg whites
    Dash of salt
¼ cup sugar
1 baked 9- or 10-inch pie shell, cooled

Combine egg yolks and 1 cup water in top of double boiler. Add ¼ cup sugar; mix well. Cook and stir over boiling water until mixture coats spoon, stirring constantly. Remove from heat, add gelatin; stir until dissolved. Add ½ cup cold water, the lemon juice, and grenadine. Chill until thickened.

Prepare whipped topping mix as directed on package. Beat egg whites and salt until foamy throughout. Add ¼ cup sugar, 2 tablespoons at a time, beating thoroughly after each addition. Continue beating until mixture will form soft, rounded peaks. Fold into gelatin mixture. Fold in 1 cup of the prepared whipped topping. Chill again, if necessary, until mixture will mound. Spoon into pie shell. Chill until firm—about 4 hours. Garnish with remaining prepared whipped topping and chocolate curls, if desired.

Centerpiece Desserts

Pretty as a flower garden, this bouquet of Fruit Tarts—and a creative pleasure to make. The Tarts are a true centerpiece dessert—attractive enough to decorate any buffet or party table. You'll also find this added grace: this is a *simplified* dessert.

Uncover more professional dessert secrets. With these Jell-O Gelatin recipes, the artist in you just naturally comes out. The Crown Jewel Cake, a *pièce-de-résistance;* the Richelieu Mold, true and dazzling elegance. Set your special table with these special desserts.

EASY FRUIT TARTS
(photographed on page 44)

> 1 package (3¼ oz.) Jell-O Vanilla
>   Pudding and Pie Filling
> 8 baked 3-inch tart shells (frozen,
>   packaged, or home baked)
> 1 to 2 cups assorted fruit (see suggested
>   fruits below)
> 1 package (3 oz.) Jell-O Strawberry,
>   Raspberry, or Orange Gelatin

Prepare pudding as directed on package; chill. Divide evenly among tart shells. Top with any of the fruit combinations below, arranging in neat design. Chill.

Meanwhile, prepare gelatin as directed on package. Chill until thickened. Spoon gelatin over tarts, using just enough to cover fruit with a smooth glaze. Chill until ready to serve. Pour remaining gelatin into serving dish and chill to use at another time. Garnish with prepared Dream Whip Whipped Topping or whipped cream, if desired. Makes 8 tarts.

Note: Recipe may be doubled for party serving, as shown in photograph.

Try these Fruits:

- Blueberries and grapes
- Blueberries and peaches
- Strawberries and green grapes
- Strawberries and bananas
- Blueberries and green grapes
- Green grapes and mandarin orange sections
- Canned pineapple slice with stemmed Bing
   Cherry in center
- Blueberries with whole strawberry in center
- Apricot halves garnished with mint sprigs
- Layered peach slices
- Whole strawberries

A beautiful fruit glaze is the secret of professional-looking continental desserts. Prepared Jell-O Gelatin, chilled until thickened but not set, can be spooned over fruit-topped pies, tarts, and puddings for an easy, flavorful glaze. After glazing, chill dessert until glaze is firm.

LAYERED PARFAIT MOLD

2　packages (3 oz. each) Jell-O Gelatin,
　　any flavor
3　cups boiling water
1　package (10 oz.) Birds Eye Quick Thaw
　　Mixed Fruit
1　pint vanilla ice cream, softened

Create new Jell-O Gelatin flavors and colors by combining two favorites, such as lemon with any red flavor, lemon with orange, raspberry with orange, lemon with orange-pineapple, and any two red flavors.

Dissolve one package gelatin in 1½ cups of the boiling water. Add mixed fruit. Stir until fruits are separated and gelatin is thickened; chill if necessary. Pour into a 6-cup ring mold. Chill until set, but not firm. Meanwhile, dissolve the remaining package of gelatin in remaining 1½ cups boiling water. Blend in softened ice cream. If necessary, chill until the gelatin is slightly thickened. Spoon over layer in mold. Chill until firm—about 4 hours. Unmold. Makes about 6 cups or 10 to 12 servings.

KEY LIME PIE
(photographed above)

    1 package (3 oz.) Jell-O Lime Gelatin
    1 cup boiling water
1 to 2 teaspoons grated lime rind
   ½ cup lime juice
    1 egg yolk, well beaten
  1⅓ cups (14 oz. can) sweetened
       condensed milk
    1 teaspoon aromatic bitters
    1 egg white
      Few drops green food coloring
       (optional)
    1 baked 9-inch pie shell, cooled

Dissolve gelatin in boiling water. Add lime rind
and juice. Pour slowly into beaten egg yolk,
stirring constantly. Add condensed milk and
bitters. Chill until slightly thickened.

Beat egg white until stiff peaks will form.
Fold into gelatin mixture. Add food coloring.
Pour into pie shell. Chill until firm—about
3 hours. Garnish with lime slices or prepared
Dream Whip Whipped Topping, if desired.

STRAWBERRY SUPREME
(photographed above)

      2 packages (3 oz.) or 1 package (6 oz.)
         Jell-O Strawberry Gelatin
    ¼ teaspoon salt
      2 cups boiling water
    1½ cups cold water
      1 package (10 oz.) Birds Eye Quick
         Thaw Strawberries
      1 cup softened vanilla ice cream
         or sour cream
    1½ tablespoons brandy
    1½ tablespoons rum
      2 tablespoons Cointreau liqueur

Dissolve gelatin and salt in boiling water. Add
cold water. Measure 2 cups into a separate
bowl. Add the frozen fruit. Stir carefully until
fruit thaws and separates. Chill until mixture is
almost set—about 15 minutes. Spoon into
sherbet glasses, filling each about two-thirds
full. Chill until set but not firm.

Chill remaining gelatin until slightly thickened.
Blend in ice cream, brandy, rum, liqueur.
Beat 1 minute or until bubbly. Spoon over gela-
tin in glasses. Chill until firm—about 3 hours.
Makes about 5½ cups or 10 servings.

CROWN JEWEL CAKE
(photographed on page 57)

>   1 package (3 oz.) Jell-O Orange Gelatin
>   1 package (3 oz.) Jell-O Cherry Gelatin
>   1 package (3 oz.) Jell-O Lime Gelatin
>   3 cups boiling water
> 1½ cups cold water
>
>   1 package (3 oz.) Jell-O Lemon Gelatin
>   ¼ cup sugar
>   1 cup boiling water
>   ½ cup canned pineapple juice
>
>   2 envelopes Dream Whip Whipped
>   Topping Mix

Cubes hold their shape best when Jell-O Gelatin is chilled overnight. To cut in cubes, use sharp knife which has been dipped in hot water. To remove cubes from pan, apply warm wet cloth over bottom of pan; then remove with spatula.

Prepare the orange, cherry, and lime gelatin separately, using 1 cup boiling water and ½ cup cold water for *each*. Pour each flavor into a separate 8-inch square pan. Chill until firm—at least 3 hours or overnight. Cut into ½-inch cubes. Set aside a few of each flavor for garnish.

Dissolve lemon gelatin and sugar in 1 cup boiling water; stir in pineapple juice. Chill until slightly thickened.

Prepare both envelopes of whipped topping mix as directed on package. Blend into the slightly thickened lemon gelatin. Fold in gelatin cubes. Spoon into 9-inch spring-form pan. Chill until firm—at least 5 hours or overnight. Just before serving, run a spatula around sides of pan; then gently remove sides. Garnish top with reserved gelatin cubes. Makes 16 servings.

Other Jewel Combinations

• Black raspberry, black cherry, and lime
   gelatin *cubes* in lemon gelatin *base*.
• Black raspberry, orange, and lime gelatin
   cubes in strawberry gelatin *base*.
• Black cherry, strawberry, and lime gelatin
   cubes in raspberry gelatin *base*.

HONEY PECAN BAVARIAN

    1 package (3 oz.) Jell-O
       Strawberry Gelatin
   ¼ teaspoon salt
    1 cup boiling water
   ⅓ cup honey
   ¼ cup cold water
    2 teaspoons lemon juice
   ½ cup light cream
   ½ cup chopped pecans

Dissolve gelatin and salt in boiling water.
Add honey, cold water, and lemon juice. Place
bowl of gelatin in a larger bowl of ice and
water, stir until slightly thickened. Beat with
rotary beater or electric mixer until fluffy
and thick, and about double in volume. Gently
stir in cream and pecans. Spoon into individual
sherbet glasses. Chill until firm—about 3
hours. Or spoon into 1 quart mold. Chill until
firm—about 4 hours. Unmold. If desired,
garnish with prepared Dream Whip Whipped
Topping and additional pecans. Makes 4 cups
or 6 to 8 servings.

MARDI GRAS MOLD

    1 package (3 oz.) Jell-O Gelatin, any
       red flavor
    1 cup boiling water
   ¾ cup cold water
    1 cup prepared Dream Whip Whipped
       Topping*
   ⅓ cup diced maraschino cherries
   ¼ cup slivered blanched almonds

*Or use ½ cup heavy cream, whipped.

Dissolve gelatin in boiling water. Add cold
water. Pour 1 cup gelatin into a 4-cup mold;
chill until set, but not firm. Chill remaining
gelatin until slightly thickened. Then fold in
whipped topping, cherries, and nuts. Carefully
spoon over the gelatin in mold. Chill until
firm—at least 4 hours. Unmold. Makes 3½
cups or 6 or 7 servings.

GRASSHOPPER DESSERT
(photographed above)

        2   packages (3 oz. each) or 1 package
              (6 oz.) Jell-O Lime Gelatin
     ¼   cup sugar
        2   cups boiling water
  1½   cups cold water
        2   tablespoons green crème de
              menthe liqueur
        1   envelope Dream Whip Whipped
              Topping Mix

Dissolve gelatin and sugar in boiling water.
Add cold water and liqueur. Pour 1 cup into a
bowl and chill until slightly thickened. Pour
remaining gelatin mixture into a 9-inch square
pan. Chill until firm—at least 3 hours. Cut into
½-inch cubes.

Meanwhile, prepare whipped topping mix as
directed on package. Blend into slightly
thickened gelatin. Pour into a 3-cup bowl.
Chill until firm—about 3 hours. Unmold
the creamy gelatin in the center of a shallow
serving bowl. Arrange gelatin cubes around the
mold. Garnish with chocolate curls, if desired.
Makes about 5 cups or 8 to 10 servings.

PEACH GEM PIE
(photographed above)

1 package (3 oz.) Jell-O Orange Gelatin
1 cup boiling water
2 cups ice cubes
½ teaspoon almond extract
2 cups sliced peeled fresh peaches
   (about 3 peaches)*
1 baked 9-inch pie shell, cooled

*Or use 1 can (16 oz.) sliced peaches, drained

Dissolve gelatin in boiling water. Add ice cubes and stir constantly until gelatin starts to thicken—3 to 5 minutes. Remove any unmelted ice. Add almond extract and peaches. Pour into pie shell. Chill until firm —about 3 hours. Garnish with whipped topping and toasted almonds, if desired.

To keep sliced fresh fruit (such as peaches, pears, and apples) from turning dark, brush with or dip in lemon juice.

BANANA NUT RING WITH GINGER TOPPING
(photographed on page 57)

2 packages (3 oz. each) Jell-O Orange or Orange-Pineapple Gelatin
2 cups boiling water
1 can (13½ oz.) pineapple tidbits or crushed pineapple
½ cup chopped pecans
2 bananas, sliced
1 envelope Dream Whip Whipped Topping Mix
2 tablespoons slivered crystallized ginger

Dissolve gelatin in boiling water. Drain pineapple, measuring syrup. Add water to syrup to make 1¾ cups; add to gelatin. Chill until thickened. Fold in pecans and bananas. Spoon into a 6-cup ring mold. Chill until firm—about 4 hours. Meanwhile, prepare whipped topping mix as directed on package; fold in drained pineapple and ginger. Chill. Unmold gelatin and spoon whipped topping mixture into center of ring mold. Garnish with pecan halves and additional ginger, if desired. Makes 5¼ cups or 10 servings.

WINTER FRUIT MOLD
(photographed on page 56)

    2 packages (3 oz. each) or 1 package
        (6 oz.) Jell-O Lemon Gelatin
    2 cups boiling water
 1½ cups cherry wine*
   15 (about) blanched almonds, halved
   ¼ teaspoon cloves
   ¼ teaspoon cinnamon
   ⅛ teaspoon allspice
    1 cup chopped candied mixed fruit
   ½ cup light raisins
   ½ cup currants
   ½ cup drained maraschino or canned
        pitted sweet cherries, halved
   ½ cup coarsely chopped walnuts

*Or use 1 bottle (12 fl. oz.) ginger ale and
1 teaspoon rum extract.

Here's an easy way to arrange fruits and vegetables in your own Jell-O Gelatin desserts and salads. Chill gelatin until thick; then pour about ¼-inch gelatin into mold. Arrange your fruits or vegetables in a decorative pattern in the gelatin. Chill until set, but not firm. Then pour remaining thickened gelatin over pattern in the mold. You can also follow this method when preparing gelatin in a shallow pan for cutting into individual servings.

Dissolve gelatin in boiling water. Stir in wine. Pour ½ cup of the mixture into a 6-cup ring mold. Chill until set, but not firm. Arrange almonds in a single layer in a decorative pattern on top of set gelatin. Pour another ½ cup of the gelatin mixture over almonds. Chill again until set, but not firm. Meanwhile, add spices, fruits, and walnuts to remaining gelatin mixture; chill until slightly thickened. Then spoon gently over gelatin in mold. Chill until firm—about 4 hours. Unmold. Serve with prepared whipped topping, if desired. Makes about 6 cups or 10 to 12 servings.

RICHELIEU MOLD
(photographed on page 56)

    1 can (16 oz.) pitted dark sweet cherries
    1 package (3 oz.) Jell-O Gelatin, any
        red flavor
    1 cup boiling water
    2 tablespoons orange juice
    ¾ cup diced orange sections,
        well drained
    1 cup Birds Eye Cool Whip Non-Dairy
        Whipped Topping, thawed, or
        prepared Dream Whip Whipped
        Topping
    ¼ cup chopped toasted almonds

Drain cherries reserving ¾ cup of the syrup.
Dissolve gelatin in boiling water. Add reserved
syrup and orange juice. Chill until thickened.
Fold in cherries and oranges. Pour into a 4-cup
mold or individual molds. Chill until firm—4
hours or overnight. Combine whipped topping,
toasted almonds. Unmold gelatin. Serve
with topping. Makes 3½ cups or 6 servings.

BRANDIED CHERRY RING

    1 can (16 oz.) pitted dark sweet cherries
    ⅓ cup brandy
    2 packages (3 oz. each) or 1 package
        (6 oz.) Jell-O Cherry Gelatin
    2 cups boiling water
    1 cup prepared Dream Whip Whipped
        Topping

Drain cherries, measuring syrup. Add water to
syrup to make 1⅓ cups. Cut cherries in half.
Heat brandy and pour over cherries; let stand
about 30 minutes. Drain, adding brandy to
measured liquid. Dissolve gelatin in boiling
water. Add measured liquid. Chill until
thickened. Add cherries to half the gelatin and
pour into a 6-cup ring mold. Chill until set but
not firm. Blend whipped topping into remaining
gelatin. Spoon into mold. Chill until firm—about
4 hours. Unmold. Makes 5¼ cups or 8 to
10 servings.

STRAWBERRY BAVARIAN PIE

(photographed on page 57)

  1 package (3 oz.) Jell-O
     Strawberry Gelatin
  1 tablespoon sugar
 ⅛ teaspoon salt
  1 cup boiling water
 ½ cup cold water
  1 package (10 oz.) Birds Eye Quick
     Thaw Strawberries
  1 cup Birds Eye Cool Whip Non-Dairy
     Whipped Topping, thawed
  1 baked 9-inch pie shell, cooled

Dissolve gelatin, sugar, and salt in boiling water. Add cold water and frozen strawberries. Stir gently until fruit thaws and separates. Chill until slightly thickened. Add whipped topping; blend until smooth. (Mixture may appear slightly curdled but will smooth out on blending.) Pour into pie shell. Chill until firm—about 4 hours. Garnish with additional whipped topping and mint leaves, if desired.

PARFAIT PIE

   1 package (3 oz.) Jell-O Orange,
     Strawberry, or Raspberry Gelatin
1¼ cups boiling water
  1 pint vanilla ice cream
  1 baked 8-inch pie shell, cooled
  1 cup prepared Dream Whip Whipped
     Topping (optional)

Dissolve gelatin in boiling water. Add ice cream by spoonfuls, stirring until melted and smooth. Pour into pie shell. Chill until firm—at least 1½ hours. Garnish with whipped topping.

ALASKA SURPRISE

> 1 package (3 oz.) Jell-O Gelatin, any red flavor
> 1 cup boiling water
> ½ cup cold ginger ale
> 1 package (3 oz.) Jell-O Gelatin, any red flavor
> 1 cup boiling water
> 1 pint vanilla ice cream, slightly softened
> 3 egg whites
> 6 tablespoons sugar

Dissolve 1 package gelatin in 1 cup boiling water. Add ginger ale. Pour into 8x4-inch loaf pan. Chill until firm—about 4 hours or overnight.

Dissolve remaining package of gelatin in 1 cup boiling water. Add ice cream, stirring until well blended. Chill, if necessary, until thickened.

Cut the clear gelatin into ½-inch cubes. Fold into the thickened gelatin. Pour into 8x4-inch loaf pan or 4-cup bowl or mold. Chill until firm—about 3 hours. Unmold onto foil-lined board—about 10x6-inches. Chill.

About ½ hour before serving, beat egg whites until foamy throughout. Add sugar, 2 tablespoons at a time, beating thoroughly after each addition. Continue beating until stiff, shiny peaks form. Completely cover sides and top of loaf with meringue, being careful to seal around the base. Place in preheated broiler until meringue is golden brown—about 1½ to 2 minutes. Makes about 4⅓ cups gelatin mixture or 8 servings.

PATRIOTIC MOLD

Red Layer
- 1 package (3 oz.) Jell-O Strawberry Gelatin
- 1⅓ cups boiling water
- 1 package (10 oz.) Birds Eye Quick Thaw Strawberries

White Layer
- 1 package (3 oz.) Jell-O Lemon Gelatin
- 1 cup boiling water
- 1 pint vanilla ice cream, slightly softened

Blue Layer
- 1 package (3 oz.) Jell-O Lemon, Black Cherry, Concord Grape or Black Raspberry Gelatin
- ¼ cup sugar
- 1 cup boiling water
- ½ cup cold water
- 1½ cups fresh, frozen or drained canned blueberries, mashed

Dissolve strawberry gelatin in 1⅓ cups boiling water. Add frozen strawberries. Stir gently until fruit thaws and separates. Chill until thickened. Pour into an 8-cup mold (star-shaped, if desired), a 9-cup Bundt pan, or straight-sided saucepan. Chill until set, but not firm.

Dissolve 1 package lemon gelatin in 1 cup boiling water. Blend in ice cream, beating until smooth. Chill until thickened. Spoon over strawberry mixture in mold. Chill until set, but not firm.

Dissolve remaining package of lemon gelatin and the sugar in 1 cup boiling water. Add ½ cup cold water; chill until thickened. Stir in blueberries and spoon over lemon ice cream mixture in mold. Chill until firm, or overnight. Unmold. Makes about 8 cups or 12 to 14 servings.

RING AROUND THE FRUIT MOLD

1 can (30 oz.) fruit cocktail
2 packages (3 oz. each) or 1 package
    (6 oz.) Strawberry or Raspberry
    Gelatin
2 cups boiling water
⅓ cup coarsely chopped nuts
½ cup miniature marshmallows
1 cup prepared Dream Whip Whipped
    Topping

Drain fruit cocktail, measuring syrup. Add water
to syrup to make 1½ cups. Dissolve gelatin
in boiling water. Add measured liquid. Pour into
a 4-cup ring mold. Chill until firm—about 4 hours.

Meanwhile, combine fruit cocktail, nuts, and
marshmallows. Fold in the whipped topping.
Chill. Unmold gelatin onto large serving
plate. Spoon most of the fruit mixture into center of ring. Use remaining fruit mixture as
garnish around base of ring. Makes about 4
cups gelatin and 4 cups fruit mixture, or 8
servings.

COFFEE CREAM DESSERT

1 package (3 oz.) Jell-O Orange Gelatin
¾ cup milk, scalded
2 tablespoons sugar
1 tablespoon Instant Maxwell House,
    Sanka Brand Decaffeinated, or
    Yuban Coffee
1½ cups crushed ice
¼ teaspoon vanilla

Combine gelatin, milk, sugar, and coffee
in blender container. Cover and blend on low
speed for 30 seconds or until gelatin is dissolved. Add crushed ice and vanilla; blend at
high speed until the ice is melted—about 30
seconds. Pour into serving glasses. Chill until
set—about 15 minutes. Makes about 2½ cups
or 4 servings.

ORANGE-PINEAPPLE BAVARIAN

1 can (11 oz.) mandarin orange sections
1 can (8¾ oz.) crushed pineapple
1 package (3 oz.) Jell-O Orange-
  Pineapple or Orange Gelatin
2 tablespoons sugar
1 cup boiling water
1 teaspoon grated orange rind
1 envelope Dream Whip Whipped
  Topping Mix

Drain fruits, measuring ¾ cup of the combined syrups. Dissolve gelatin and sugar in boiling water. Add orange rind and measured syrup. Chill until slightly thickened. Prepare whipped topping mix as directed on package; blend 1½ cups into the gelatin mixture. Chill until thickened. Fold in fruits. Pour into 5-cup mold. Chill until firm—at least 4 hours. Unmold and garnish with remaining prepared whipped topping. Makes about 5 cups or about 8 servings.

Salads that Help Make the Meal

Cool, fresh, and colorful as a greenhouse, this Green Goddess Salad Bowl—one of the main dish salads that turn out so well with Jell-O Gelatin.

With these recipes, you'll find some hints to make your salads successful every time. Serve Under-the-Sea Pear Salad at your weekend brunch, or prepare smooth jellied Chicken Mousse ahead of time. It will stay fresh and firm in the refrigerator until the mixed doubles players return after the tennis match.

With little effort, you can delight everyone with your cool and colorful Jell-O Gelatin salads. So good they practically make the meal.

GREEN GODDESS SALAD BOWL
(photographed on page 64)

  - 2 packages (3 oz. each) or 1 package (6 oz.) Jell-O Lime Gelatin
  - 1 tablespoon garlic salt
  - 1 teaspoon salt
    Dash of pepper
  - 2 cups boiling water
  - 1½ cups sour cream
  - ½ cup mayonnaise
  - 2 tablespoons vinegar
  - 2 cans (2 oz. each) anchovies, finely chopped

  - 2 quarts bite size pieces salad greens
  - 2 cans (7½ oz. each) crab meat
  - 2 avocados, peeled and sliced

Dissolve gelatin, garlic salt, salt, and pepper in boiling water. Add sour cream, mayonnaise, vinegar, and anchovies. Beat until well blended. Pour into two 8-inch square pans. Chill until firm—at least one hour. Just before serving, cut gelatin into small cubes, about ½ inch square. Pile gelatin cubes in center of shallow bowl; arrange salad greens, crabmeat and avocado around edge. Makes 8 entree servings.

JELLIED SALAD NICOISE

1 can (7 oz.) tuna, drained and coarsely
　flaked
1 small tomato, diced and drained
½ cup cooked cut green beans (optional)
2 tablespoons sliced ripe olives
2 tablespoons green pepper strips
2 tablespoons red onion strips
2 tablespoons mild French or Italian
　dressing
1 package (3 oz.) Jell-O Lemon Gelatin
1 teaspoon salt
1 cup boiling water
½ cup cold water
2 teaspoons vinegar
1 hard-cooked egg, diced
2 cups coarsely chopped lettuce

½ cup mayonnaise
2 tablespoons cream or milk
2 anchovy fillets, finely chopped
　(optional)

Combine tuna, vegetables, and French dressing in a bowl. Mix lightly; let stand while preparing gelatin mixture.

Dissolve gelatin and salt in boiling water.
Add cold water and vinegar. Chill until mixture just begins to thicken. Then spoon vegetable mixture and diced egg into a 6-cup ring mold. Pour on half the gelatin. Spread lettuce on top. Add remaining gelatin. Chill until firm—at least 4 hours.

Mix mayonnaise, cream, and anchovies. Unmold salad. Garnish with watercress, if desired. Serve with mayonnaise dressing. Makes about 5 cups or 6 entree salads.

ANTIPASTO SALAD
(photographed above)

    1 package (3 oz.) Jell-O Lemon Gelatin
    1 teaspoon salt
    1 cup boiling water
    1 tablespoon vinegar
    2 cup ice cubes
    ½ cup finely cut salami
    ⅓ cup finely cut Swiss cheese
    ¼ cup chopped celery
    ¼ cup chopped onion
    2 tablespoons sliced ripe olives

Dissolve gelatin and salt in boiling water. Add vinegar and ice cubes; stir constantly until thickened—about 3 minutes. Remove any unmelted ice. Stir in remaining ingredients. Pour into a 3-cup serving bowl and chill until firm—about 3 hours. Makes 2½ cups or 4 servings.

Note: Recipe may be doubled.

UNDER-THE-SEA PEAR SALAD
(photographed above)

- 1 can (16 oz.) pear halves
- 1 package (3 oz.) Jell-O Lime Gelatin
- ¼ teaspoon salt
- 1 cup boiling water
- 1 tablespoon lemon juice
- 2 packages (3 oz. each) cream cheese
- ⅛ teaspoon ginger

Drain pears, reserving ¾ cup of the syrup. Coarsely dice pears and set aside. Dissolve gelatin and salt in boiling water. Add pear syrup and lemon juice. Measure 1¼ cups into an 8x4-inch loaf pan or a 4-cup mold. Chill until set, but not firm—about 1 hour.

Meanwhile, soften cheese until creamy. Very slowly blend in remaining gelatin, beating until smooth. Blend in ginger. Stir in pears. Spoon over set gelatin in pan. Chill until firm—about 4 hours. Unmold and garnish with chicory or watercress. Serve with mayonnaise, if desired. Makes about 3½ cups or 6 servings.

Note: Recipe may be doubled, using a 9x5-inch loaf pan.

GARDEN SOUFFLÉ SALAD

- 1 package (3 oz.) Jell-O Lemon or Lime Gelatin
- ¼ teaspoon salt
- 1 cup boiling water
- ½ cup cold water
- ¼ cup mayonnaise
- 1 to 2 tablespoons vinegar or lemon juice
- 1 tablespoon grated onion
  Dash of pepper
- ⅓ cup *each* diced raw cauliflower, shredded carrots, sliced radishes, diced celery, and chopped watercress
- 2 tablespoons diced green pepper

Dissolve gelatin and salt in boiling water. Add cold water, mayonnaise, vinegar, onion, and pepper. Beat until well blended. Pour into an 8-inch square pan. Freeze 15 to 20 minutes, or until firm about 1 inch from edge, but soft in center.

Spoon mixture into bowl and whip until fluffy. Fold in vegetables. Pour into 4-cup mold or individual molds. Chill in refrigerator (*not* freezing unit) until firm—30 to 60 minutes. Unmold. Garnish with salad greens and serve with additional mayonnaise, if desired. Makes 4 cups or 8 servings.

TURKEY-SOUFFLE SALAD

1 package (3 oz.) Jell-O Lemon or Lime Gelatin
¼ teaspoon salt
1 cup boiling water
½ cup cold water
¼ cup mayonnaise
1 to 2 tablespoons vinegar or lemon juice
1 tablespoon grated onion
Dash of pepper
1½ cups diced cooked turkey
⅓ cup chopped cucumber or green pepper
⅓ cup chopped celery
2 tablespoons chopped pimiento

Dissolve gelatin and salt in boiling water. Add cold water, mayonnaise, vinegar, onion and pepper. Beat until well blended. Pour into an 8-inch square pan. Freeze 15 to 20 minutes, or until firm about 1 inch from edge but soft in center.

Spoon mixture into bowl and whip until fluffy. Fold in turkey and chopped vegetables. Pour into 4-cup mold or individual molds. Chill in refrigerator (*not* freezing unit) until firm—30 to 60 minutes. Unmold. Garnish with salad greens and serve with additional mayonnaise, if desired. Makes about 4 cups or 4 entree servings.

CHICKEN MOUSSE
(photographed on pages 72-73)

3 cups chicken broth*
2 packages (3 oz. each) or 1 package
      (6 oz.) Jell-O Lemon Gelatin
1 teaspoon salt
⅛ teaspoon cayenne
3 tablespoons vinegar
1⅓ cups prepared Dream Whip Whipped
      Topping Mix
⅔ cup mayonnaise
2 cups finely diced cooked chicken
2 cups finely chopped celery
2 tablespoons chopped pimiento

*Or use 3 chicken bouillon cubes dissolved
in 3 cups boiling water.

Bring 2 cups of the broth to a boil. Pour over
gelatin, salt, and cayenne, stirring until gelatin
is dissolved. Add remaining broth and the
vinegar. Chill until slightly thickened.

Meanwhile, blend together whipped topping
and mayonnaise. Fold in chicken, celery, and
pimiento and chill. Fold thickened gelatin
into chicken mixture, blending well. Spoon into
a 9x5-inch loaf pan. Chill until firm—about 6
hours or overnight. Unmold.

Garnish with crisp lettuce, additional mayonnaise, and stuffed olives, if desired. Makes 7
cups or 6 entree salads.

FLORIDA SEACOAST SALAD

1 package (3 oz.) Jell-O Lemon Gelatin
1 teaspoon salt
½ teaspoon garlic salt
1 cup boiling water
½ cup cold water
1 tablespoon vinegar
⅛ teaspoon pepper
1 cup diced cooked shrimp
1 package (9 oz.) Birds Eye Deluxe
    Artichoke Hearts
1 cup prepared Good Seasons Garlic
    Salad Dressing
1 grapefruit, sectioned
1 orange, sectioned
1 large avocado, peeled and diced
1 cup thin strips Cheddar cheese
¼ cup chopped green onions
3 quarts salad greens (lettuce, romaine,
    escarole, Chinese cabbage,
    watercress)

Dissolve gelatin, salt, and garlic salt in boiling water. Add cold water, vinegar and pepper. Chill until thickened. Pour into 8x4-inch loaf pan. Arrange small groups of diced shrimp 1 inch apart. Chill until firm—about 3 hours. Cut in 1-inch squares.

Meanwhile, cook artichokes as directed on the package. Drain; then cut each in half. Add salad dressing. Chill.

Combine remaining ingredients in large salad bowl; chill. Just before serving add marinated artichokes. Toss together lightly. Arrange gelatin squares on top. Makes about 6 cups or 6 entree salads.

Sociable Side Salads

Add a refreshing touch to any entree with a special Jell-O Gelatin side salad. With little effort, you can make an ordinary meal spectacular with the addition of such a cool dish. In the dreary stretches of winter, when greens may be scarce and expensive, refreshing jellied salads can be made with winter apples and nuts, grapefruit and oranges, or canned cranberry sauce and apples.

These side salads can also double as appetizers. The Jellied Gazpacho, pictured opposite, for example, is a flavorful vegetable-filled first course for a picnic supper or family dinner.

Jell-O Gelatin sociable side salads can be molded, spooned, or cut into squares. And in every form, they add sparkle to your family meals.

JELLIED GAZPACHO
(photographed on page 76)

>   2 cups finely chopped tomatoes
>   ½ cup finely chopped green pepper
>   ½ cup finely chopped celery
>   ½ cup finely chopped onion
>   1 can (4 oz.) sliced mushrooms, drained
>   and finely chopped
>   1 tablespoon finely chopped parsley
>   1 teaspoon finely chopped chives
> 1½ teaspoons garlic salt
> 1½ teaspoons salt
>   ¼ teaspoon pepper
>   2 tablespoons tarragon vinegar
>   ¼ teaspoon pepper sauce
>   Dash of Worcestershire sauce
>
>   2 packages (3 oz. each) or
>   1 package (6 oz.) Jell-O
>   Lemon Gelatin
>   2 cups boiling water
> 1½ cups cold water

Combine all vegetables, seasonings, the vinegar, pepper sauce, and Worcestershire sauce. Let stand.

Dissolve gelatin in boiling water. Stir in cold water. Chill until thickened. Stir in vegetable mixture. Chill in large bowl or tureen until set, but not firm. Garnish with chopped tomatoes and cucumbers, if desired. Makes about 6½ cups or 8 to 10 servings.

Note: Gazpacho may be chilled overnight. Break up with fork before serving.

Since metal chills more quickly than glass, Jell-O Gelatin in metal bowls will be firm in less time than Jell-O Gelatin in a glass mixing bowl or in a glass serving dish.

SNAPPY FRUIT MOLD

 1 package (3 oz.) Jell-O Gelatin, any red flavor
 ⅛ teaspoon salt
 ¾ cup boiling water
 1 can (8 oz.) jellied cranberry sauce
 1 tablespoon grated orange rind
 1 medium tart apple, finely chopped (about 1 cup)
 ⅓ cup chopped nuts
  Whipped Cream Mayonnaise

Dissolve gelatin and salt in boiling water. Stir cranberry sauce with fork until smooth. Add to gelatin with orange rind, blending well. Chill until thickened. Add apples and nuts. Pour into a 3-cup mold or 5 individual molds. Chill until firm—about 4 hours. Unmold. Garnish with Whipped Cream Mayonnaise and additional chopped nuts, if desired. Makes 2½ cups or 5 individual salads.

Note: Recipe may be doubled.

WHIPPED CREAM MAYONNAISE

Whip ½ cup heavy cream. Fold in ¼ cup mayonnaise and ⅛ teaspoon salt. Makes about 1¼ cups.

BARBECUE SALAD

 1 package (3 oz.) Jell-O Lemon, Orange, or Orange-Pineapple Gelatin
 1 cup boiling water
 1 can (8 oz.) tomato sauce
 1½ tablespoons vinegar
 ½ teaspoon salt
  Dash of pepper

Dissolve gelatin in boiling water. Add remaining ingredients. Blend. Pour into individual molds or a 3-cup mold. Chill until firm—about 4 hours. Unmold. Serve on crisp salad greens with mayonnaise, if desired. Makes about 2 cups or 4 servings.

ZESTY GINGER-FRUIT SALAD
(photographed above)

> 1 package (3 oz.) Jell-O Orange Gelatin
> ¼ teaspoon ground ginger
> ⅛ teaspoon salt
> 1 cup boiling water
> 1 bottle (7 fl. oz.) ginger ale
> ¾ cup fresh orange sections, halved
> ¾ cup fresh grapefruit sections, halved

Dissolve gelatin, ginger, and salt in boiling water. Add ginger ale. Place bowl with 1 cup of gelatin in larger bowl of ice and water, stir until slightly thickened. Whip with electric mixer or rotary beater until mixture is fluffy and thick and about double in volume. Pour into an 8-inch square pan. Chill until set, but not firm.

Chill remaining gelatin until thickened. Fold in orange and grapefruit sections. Spoon gently over set gelatin. Chill until firm—about 4 hours. Cut into squares. Serve with crisp greens. Makes about 4 cups or 6 to 8 servings.

When chilling gelatin mixture in ice bath, stir occasionally to insure even thickening.

To keep gelatin salads cool and firm, always serve on chilled plates.

JELLIED FRESH VEGETABLE SALAD
(photographed above)

- 1 package (3 oz.) Jell-O Lemon Gelatin
- 2 bouillon cubes
- ½ teaspoon salt
- 1 cup boiling water
- 2 tablespoons tarragon vinegar
  Dash of pepper
- 1 cup sour cream
- ½ cup diced celery
- ⅓ cup thinly sliced radishes
- ⅓ cup diced cucumber
- 2 tablespoons green pepper strips
- 2 tablespoons thinly sliced scallions

Dissolve gelatin, bouillon cubes, and salt in boiling water. Add vinegar and pepper. Chill until slightly thickened. Blend in sour cream and add remaining ingredients. Pour into a 3-cup mold or individual molds. Chill until firm —about 4 hours. Unmold and garnish with crisp lettuce or chicory. Serve with French dressing or mayonnaise, if desired. Makes 2¾ cups or 5 or 6 servings.

CUCUMBER-SOUR CREAM MOLD

- 2 medium cucumbers, peeled and coarsely grated (about 1½ cups)
- 1 package (3 oz.) Jell-O Lemon or Lime Gelatin
- 1 teaspoon salt
- 1 cup boiling water
- ¾ cup cold water
- 2 teaspoons vinegar
- ½ cup sour cream
- 1 tablespoon chopped onion
- 1 tablespoon chopped parsley
- ⅛ teaspoon coarsely ground black pepper

Wrap grated cucumbers in a clean cloth or absorbent paper and squeeze tightly to remove juice. *Let drain completely.* Meanwhile, dissolve gelatin and salt in boiling water. Add cold water and vinegar. Blend in sour cream. Chill until thickened. Fold in drained cucumbers, onion, parsley, and pepper. Pour into a 4-cup mold or individual molds. Chill until firm—about 4 hours. Makes about 3⅔ cups or 6 servings.

JELLIED WALDORF SALAD

- 1 package (3 oz.) Jell-O Orange Gelatin Dash of salt
- 1 cup boiling water
- ¾ cup cold water
- 1 tablespoon lemon juice
- ¾ cup diced unpeeled apple
- ¼ cup chopped celery
- ¼ cup chopped nuts

Dissolve gelatin and salt in boiling water. Add cold water and lemon juice. Chill until thickened. Stir in remaining ingredients. Pour into a 4-cup mold. Chill until firm—about 4 hours. Unmold. Garnish with crisp salad greens. Serve with mayonnaise, thinned with cream or honey, if desired. Makes about 3 cups or 6 servings.

COOL COLESLAW SALAD

> 1 package (3 oz.) Jell-O Orange-Pineapple or Lemon Gelatin
> ½ teaspoon salt
> 1 cup boiling water
> ½ cup cold water
> 2 tablespoons vinegar
> ½ cup mayonnaise
> ½ cup sour cream
> 1 tablespoon prepared mustard
> 1 teaspoon grated onion
> 3 cups shredded cabbage
> 2 tablespoons diced pimiento
> 1 tablespoon chopped parsley

Dissolve gelatin and salt in boiling water. Add vinegar, cold water and stir in mayonnaise, sour cream, mustard, and onion, blending thoroughly. Chill until thickened. Fold in cabbage, pimiento, and parsley. Pour into glass or china serving bowl; chill until firm—about 2 hours. Makes 4 cups or 6 to 8 servings.

CARROT, CELERY, AND OLIVE SALAD

> 1 package (3 oz.) Jell-O Lemon or Lime Gelatin
> ¼ teaspoon salt
> 1 cup boiling water
> ¾ cup cold water
> 2 teaspoons vinegar
> 1 cup shredded carrots
> ¼ cup diced celery
> 2 tablespoons sliced olives

Dissolve gelatin and salt in boiling water. Add cold water and vinegar. Chill until thickened. Stir in carrots, celery, and olives. Spoon into a 4-cup mold or individual molds. Chill until firm—about 4 hours. Unmold. Garnish with crisp salad greens. If desired, serve with mayonnaise. Makes 2½ cups or 5 servings.

Salads for the Slim Life

Keeping fit is a sociable activity these days. Friends gather together for a weekend of skiing. Mother and daughter work out in the same exercise class. Father takes up early morning jogging. Even keep-fit meals are shared with friends and family.

Jell-O Gelatin salads fit neatly into these menus for waistline watchers. The sparkling gelatin adds appetite appeal to such foods as chopped raw vegetables, fresh fruit, diced chicken, and hard-cooked eggs. (A half-cup serving of plain Jell-O Gelatin, by the way, checks in at about 80 calories.)

These keep-fit recipes are expanded to complete salad plates that fill nutrition needs for lunch or brunch or supper. Each *complete salad plate* accounts for under 350 calories. Enjoy the delicious way to maintain a slim life with these Jell-O Gelatin salads.

MOLDED HAM AND EGG SALAD
(photographed on page 84)

        2 packages (3 oz. each) or 1 package
              (6 oz.) Jell-O Lemon Gelatin
      ½ teaspoon salt
        2 cups boiling water
    1½ cups cold water
        2 tablespoons vinegar
        2 hard-cooked eggs, sliced
        2 cups finely diced cooked ham
        1 cup finely chopped celery
        2 tablespoons finely chopped onion
        1 hard-cooked egg, chopped

Dissolve gelatin and salt in boiling water. Add cold water and vinegar. Set aside ½ cup. Chill remaining gelatin until slightly thickened—about 1 hour. Pour reserved gelatin into an 8x4-inch loaf pan. Chill until set, but not firm—about 15 minutes.

Arrange egg slices on set gelatin. Fold ham, celery, onion and chopped egg into slightly thickened gelatin. Spoon carefully onto gelatin in pan. Chill until firm—about 6 hours or over-night. Unmold. Garnish with salad greens. Makes 5¾ cups or 5 or 6 servings.

Note: The glazed sliced egg decoration may be omitted. For a simplified version, dissolve gelatin and salt in boiling water, add cold water and vinegar. Chill until thickened, fold in remaining ingredients, pour into pan, and chill until firm. Garnish with the 2 sliced hard-cooked eggs.

Keep Fit Salad Luncheon Platter

Serve Ham and Egg Salad Mold and 2 thin slices tomato on Boston lettuce with an appetizer of chicken broth. (About 350 calories.)

JELLIED TURKEY SALAD

>   1 package (3 oz.) Jell-O Lemon Gelatin
>   1 teaspoon salt
>   1 cup boiling water
>   ¾ cup cold water
>   2 teaspoons lemon juice
>   1 cup diced cooked turkey or chicken
>   ¼ pound red or black grapes, halved and
>   seeded (about ¾ cup)
>   ½ cup diced celery
>   ⅛ teaspoon tarragon leaves

Dissolve gelatin and salt in boiling water. Add cold water and lemon juice. Chill until thickened. Stir in remaining ingredients. Spoon into 4-cup mold or individual molds. Chill until firm —about 4 hours. Unmold. Garnish with crisp greens and watercress, if desired. Makes about 3½ cups or 4 salads.

Jellied Turkey Platter

Serve about 1 cup well-seasoned Jellied Turkey Salad on romaine. Add ¼ cup cottage cheese sprinkled with celery salt and garnished with 2 green pepper strips and 5 thin carrot sticks. Serve with 1 teaspoon low calorie French dressing. (About 235 calories.)

SPANISH TUNA SALAD
(photographed on pages 88-89)

2 packages (3 oz. each) or 1 package
(6 oz.) Jell-O Lemon Gelatin
1 tablespoon salt
2 cups boiling water
1¼ cups cold water
3 tablespoons vinegar
⅛ teaspoon pepper
½ cup diced tomato
¼ cup small thin strips unpeeled
cucumber
¼ cup coarsely chopped celery
2 tablespoons chopped scallion or
onion
1 can (7 oz.) tuna, well drained and
broken in chunks

Dissolve gelatin, and salt, in boiling water. Add
cold water and vinegar and pepper. Chill until
thickened. Add remaining ingredients. Pour into a 5- or 6-cup mold or individual 1 cup molds.
Chill until firm—at least 4 hours or overnight.
Unmold. Serve with mayonnaise, if desired. (For
lower calorie platter, substitute a squeeze of
lemon for dressing.) Makes about 5 cups or 5
servings.

Spanish Tuna Salad Luncheon Platter

Serve 1 cup Spanish Tuna Salad on lettuce
with 1 hard cooked egg and 2 small radishes.
(About 300 calories.)

QUICK CRANBERRY-APPLE MOLD

- 1 package (3 oz.) Jell-O Raspberry or Strawberry Gelatin
- ⅓ cup sugar
- ⅛ teaspoon salt
- ⅛ teaspoon cinnamon
  Dash of ground cloves
- ¾ cup boiling water
- 1 cup crushed ice
- 1 medium apple, peeled, cored, and cut into wedges
- 1 cup fresh cranberries

Combine gelatin, sugar, spices, and boiling water in an electric blender container. Cover; blend at low speed until gelatin is dissolved—about 30 seconds. Add crushed ice and blend at high speed until ice is melted—about 30 seconds. Measure out 3 cups of gelatin mixture and chill until thickened. Add apple wedges and cranberries to the remaining gelatin in blender and blend at low speed until fruit is broken into pieces; stir into thickened gelatin. Pour mixture into a 4-cup mold or individual molds and chill until firm—about 1 hour. Unmold. Makes 4 cups or 8 servings.

Quick Chicken Cranberry Mold Platter

Serve two or three slices white meat of chicken with ½ cup Quick Cranberry Mold on lettuce with 2 slices party rye bread and 2 cucumber strips. (About 300 calories.)

Salads for Special Events

Lucky is the bride who has her reception prepared by the loving hands of family and friends.

If a wedding reception, shower, anniversary party, birthday celebration, open house, or other special event are on *your* schedule, consider serving several colorful jellied salads. Offer a tempting variety, such as the salmon, fresh fruit, and tangy cheese salads photographed on the opposite page. All can be prepared ahead of time and kept well-chilled until serving.

Big parties have a share-and-help mood about them these days, so get friends together and let the salad making become a special event itself. Begin it all with Jell-O Gelatin.

FRESH FRUIT SALAD
(photographed on page 92)

     1   package (3 oz.) Jell-O Lemon Gelatin
    1¼   cups boiling water
     ⅔   cup sour cream
     ⅓   cup mayonnaise
     1   tablespoon sugar
     2   teaspoons lemon juice
     2   cups coarsely chopped peeled apples
     1   cup halved seedless or pitted green
          grapes
     ¼   cup chopped pecans
     1   package (3 oz.) Jell-O Orange Gelatin
     1   cup boiling water
     ¾   cup cold water

Dissolve lemon gelatin in 1¼ cups boiling
water; cool slightly. Combine sour cream,
mayonnaise, sugar, and lemon juice; stir in
apples, grapes, and pecans. Blend sour cream
mixture into lemon gelatin. Chill until slightly
thickened—about 1 hour.

Meanwhile, dissolve orange gelatin in 1 cup
boiling water. Add cold water. Pour ⅔ cup into
a 6-cup ring mold; chill until set but not firm—
about 30 minutes. Chill remaining orange
gelatin until slightly thickened. Spoon lemon
gelatin fruit mixture over orange gelatin in
mold and top with remaining orange gelatin.
Chill until firm—about 4 hours or overnight.
Makes about 6 cups or 12 servings.

CREAMY BLEU CHEESE SALAD
(photographed on page 92)

          2 packages (3 oz. each) or 1 package
             (6 oz.) Jell-O Lemon Gelatin
          1 teaspoon salt
          2 cups boiling water
       1½ cups cold water
          2 packages (3 oz. each) cream cheese,
             softened
          ½ cup crumbled bleu cheese
          ½ teaspoon paprika
          1 envelope Dream Whip Whipped
             Topping

For storage overnight or longer, it is wise to cover Jell-O Gelatin to prevent evaporation and drying.

Dissolve gelatin and salt in boiling water. Add cold water. Chill until slightly thickened. Blend cream cheese with bleu cheese and paprika. Add gelatin gradually and beat until thoroughly blended. Prepare whipped topping as directed on package; fold into gelatin mixture. Spoon into individual molds or a 7- or 8-cup mold. Chill until firm—3 hours or overnight. Unmold. Serve with crisp salad greens. Garnish with fresh fruit, if desired. Makes 7 cups or 12 to 14 servings.

SALMON DILL MOUSSE
(photographed on page 92)

          2 packages (3 oz. each) or 1 package
             (6 oz.) Jell-O Lemon Gelatin
          2 cups boiling water
          1 cup cold water
          3 tablespoons lemon juice
          1 can (1 lb.) pink salmon, drained
             and flaked
          ½ cup sour cream
          ¼ cup mayonnaise
          2 tablespoons minced onion
       1½ teaspoons dill weed

Dissolve gelatin in boiling water. Add cold water and lemon juice. Chill until thickened. Mix salmon with remaining ingredients. Blend into thickened gelatin. Pour into an 8x4-inch loaf pan. Chill until firm—about 4 hours. Unmold. Garnish with dill and thinly-sliced cucumber, if desired. Makes 5⅓ cups or 6 to 8 servings.

ARTICHOKE SALAD

    1 package (9 oz.) Birds Eye Deluxe
          Artichoke Hearts
    1 cup (about ¼ lb.) sliced fresh
          mushrooms
    1 cup prepared Good Seasons Italian
          Salad Dressing

    1 package (3 oz.) Jell-O Lemon or Lime
          Gelatin
    1 cup boiling water
    2 teaspoons vinegar
    ¾ cup cold water
    1 tablespoon sliced pimiento

Cook artichoke hearts as directed on package.
Drain and combine with mushrooms in a bowl.
Pour dressing over vegetables and allow to
marinate—at least 1 hour. Drain, reserving
marinade.

Dissolve gelatin in boiling water. Add vinegar
and cold water. Chill until thickened. Fold in the
drained mushrooms and artichoke hearts, and
the pimiento. Pour into a 4-cup mold. Chill until
firm—about 4 hours. Makes 3⅓ cups or 6
salads.

Note: If desired, reserved marinade can be
combined with mayonnaise and used as a
dressing for the salad.

MOLDED POTATO SALAD

3 to 4 tablespoons vinegar
1 envelope Good Seasons Mild Italian
Salad Dressing Mix
4 cups sliced or diced cold cooked
potatoes
2 strips crisp fried bacon, finely
crumbled
1 package (3 oz.) Jell-O Lemon Gelatin
1 cup boiling water
¼ cup cold water
2 cups mayonnaise

To hasten chilling, chill
the filled mold about
ten minutes in a pan of
ice and water before
placing in refrigerator.

Combine vinegar and salad dressing mix. Add
to potatoes and bacon. Chill about 1 hour.
Dissolve gelatin in boiling water; add cold
water. Blend in mayonnaise. Chill until thickened. Add potato mixture. Pour into 6-cup
mold. Chill until firm—about 4 hours. Unmold.
Makes about 6 cups or 8 servings.

SEQUIN SALAD

2 packages (3 oz. each) or 1 package
(6 oz.) Jell-O Lime Gelatin
2 cups boiling water
1½ cups cold water
3 tablespoons vinegar
2 teaspoons salt
⅛ teaspoon pepper
¼ cup grated onion
2½ cups very small pieces raw cauliflower
½ cup diced pimiento

Dissolve gelatin in boiling water. Add cold
water. Chill until thickened. Meanwhile, mix
vinegar, salt, and pepper together in small
bowl; add onion, cauliflower, and pimiento. Let
stand to blend; fold into thickened gelatin.
Pour into individual molds or 6-cup mold.
Chill until firm—at least 1 hour for individual
molds or 4 hours for large mold. Unmold. Serve
with mayonnaise or French dressing, if desired. Makes 8 to 10 servings.

LAYERED CRANBERRY-APPLE MOLD

         2   packages (3 oz. each) or 1 package
             (6 oz.) Jell-O Lemon Gelatin
        ¼   cup sugar
        ¼   teaspoon salt
         2   cups boiling water
      1½   cups cranberry-apple drink
         1   can (8 oz.) whole berry cranberry
             sauce
         2   cups (or one 4½-oz. container)
             Birds Eye Cool Whip Non-Dairy
             Whipped Topping, thawed
        ¼   cup mayonnaise
         1   unpeeled apple, cored and finely diced

Dissolve gelatin, sugar, and salt in boiling
water. Add cranberry-apple drink. Set aside 2
cups gelatin mixture. Blend cranberry sauce
into remaining gelatin mixture. Chill until thickened. Pour into an 8-cup ring mold. Chill until set, but not firm. Meanwhile, chill the reserved
2 cups gelatin mixture until thickened. Blend
in whipped topping and mayonnaise. Add apple. Spoon over first layer in mold. Chill until
firm—at least 6 hours or overnight. Unmold. Garnish with crisp salad greens. Makes about 7½
cups or 12 to 14 servings.

JELLIED AVOCADO RING

         4   packages (3 oz. each) or 2 packages
             (6 oz. each) Jell-O Lime Gelatin
      1½   teaspoons salt
         4   cups boiling water
         3   cups cold water
        ¼   cup lemon juice
         4   ripe avocados, peeled and mashed
        ¾   cup mayonnaise

Dissolve gelatin and salt in boiling water. Add
cold water. Chill until thickened. Stir lemon
juice into avocados. Stir avocado mixture and
mayonnaise into gelatin mixture, blending
well. Pour into a 12-cup ring mold. Chill until
firm—at least 6 hours or overnight. Unmold.
Makes about 10 cups or 20 servings.

MOLDED VEGETABLE RELISH

        1 package (3 oz.) Jell-O Lemon or
            Lime Gelatin
        ¾ teaspoon salt
        1 cup boiling water
        ¾ cup cold water
        2 tablespoons vinegar
        2 teaspoons grated onion
            Dash of pepper
            Vegetable Combinations*

Dissolve gelatin and salt in boiling water. Add cold water, vinegar, grated onion, and pepper. Chill until thickened. Fold in vegetable combination. Pour into individual molds for salad or small molds for relish. Chill until firm—about 3 hours. Unmold. For salad, serve with crisp lettuce and garnish with mayonnaise, if desired. Makes about 3 cups or 6 salad servings or 8 relish servings.

Vegetable Combinations

— ½ cup *each* finely chopped cabbage, celery, and carrots, and 3 tablespoons finely chopped green pepper.

— ¾ cup *each* finely chopped cabbage and celery, ¼ cup finely chopped green pepper, and 2 tablespoons diced pimiento.

— ¾ cup *each* finely chopped cabbage and celery, ½ cup chopped pickle, and 2 tablespoons diced pimiento.

— ¾ cup *each* drained cooked peas and diced celery and ½ cup finely chopped cabbage.

— 1 cup finely chopped cabbage, ½ cup sliced stuffed olives, and omit the salt.

— ⅔ cup grated carrots and ¼ cup finely chopped green pepper.

Especially for Junior Cooks

Jell-O Gelatin is a *young* dessert. Cool and sparkling. Fresh and fruity. And the colors are pure pop art. (Next time you pour boiling water on the powdered gelatin, just watch those colors come alive.)

Jell-O Gelatin desserts are easy and quick to prepare, too. Another reason for starting your cooking career with these ideas. A few minutes of mixing and pouring and you have a beautiful dessert to chill and carry to the table.

Let it be fun—something to share with people you love. Invite a special friend, or your younger sister, to help you make Supersodas. Share your Snack Cups with a hungry Dad.

Begin in a big way. Start with Jell-O Gelatin.

POP ART PARFAITS

Start with Jell-O Gelatin, follow the easy package directions, then go on to create parfaits in shimmering pop art colors and designs. Make your creations in glass mugs, tall iced tea glasses, parfait glasses, soda glasses—even water goblets. Make your own masterpieces, or try these delicious designs.

COOL CUBES—Prepare Jellied Cubes as directed on page 12, using Jell-O Orange Gelatin. In tall glasses, alternate cubes with canned, drained, chilled mandarin orange sections.

DREAM PARFAIT—Prepare Jell-O Strawberry Gelatin as directed on package, and chill until very thick and jiggly. Meanwhile, prepare Dream Whip Whipped Topping Mix as directed on package. Layer gelatin and prepared whipped topping in parfait glasses, ending with topping.

KICKY COOLER—Prepare Jell-O Strawberry Gelatin as directed on package; pour into sherbet or parfait glasses. Chill until set—about 3 hours, then top with scoop of ice cream.

RAINBOW PARFAIT—Prepare Jell-O Lemon Gelatin and Jell-O Raspberry Gelatin as directed on package, chilling until slightly thickened. Layer gelatin in tall or parfait glasses, chilling each layer until set, but not firm before adding the next layer. Chill until firm—about 3 hours. When ready to serve, you might like to add a final pop art garnish —a few small green grapes on each serving.

BANANA-MARSHMALLOW SPECIAL

Here's a refreshing, fruit-filled dessert that you can make your own specialty.

What you need

     1 package (3 oz.) Jell-O
       Strawberry Gelatin
     1 cup boiling water
    ¾ cup cold water
     1 cup sliced bananas
    1½ cups miniature marshmallows

What you do

1. Dissolve gelatin in boiling water in a medium bowl. Stir until all the gelatin is dissolved. Then add cold water and stir. Chill until almost set (to keep marshmallows from all popping to the top later).

2. Gently fold in bananas and marshmallows. Pour (or spoon) into 6 glasses, dishes, or paper cups. Chill until firm—about 3 hours. Makes about 3 cups or 6 servings.

JIFFY COOLER

Stir up this delicious, pastel dessert, have it chilled and ready to eat in an hour!

What you need

1 package (3 oz.) Jell-O Gelatin,
    any red flavor
1 cup boiling water
1 cup cold water
1 pint vanilla ice cream

What you do

1. Dissolve gelatin in boiling water in a large bowl. Stir until all the gelatin is dissolved. Then add cold water to gelatin mixture and stir.

2. Add ice cream by spoonfuls, stirring until melted. Pour into serving bowl. Chill until slightly thickened—about 30 minutes.

3. Stir for a few seconds, then chill until firm—about 30 minutes more. Makes about 3½ cups or 4 servings.

SUPERSODAS

Set up your own ice cream parlor with a row of Supersodas, all cool and beautiful.

What you need

1 package (3 oz.) Jell-O Concord Grape, Cherry, Strawberry, or Raspberry Gelatin
1 cup boiling water
1 cup club soda
¼ cup cold water
½ pint vanilla ice cream
Prepared Dream Whip Whipped Topping

What you do

1. Dissolve gelatin in boiling water in a large bowl. Stir until all gelatin is dissolved. Add club soda and cold water. Chill in refrigerator until slightly thickened. Measure one cup of the thickened gelatin into a small bowl and set aside.

2. Place a scoop of ice cream in each of 3 tall iced tea or soda glasses. Fill the glasses two-thirds full with slightly thickened gelatin from large bowl.

3. Then use rotary beater or electric mixer to whip the gelatin in small bowl until light and fluffy. Fill the remainder of each glass with whipped gelatin.

4. Chill sodas until firm—about 2 hours. Before serving, decorate with a dollop or swirl of prepared whipped topping. Or pass the topping in a small bowl and let everyone add their own fancy touch. Makes about three 12-oz. sodas.

SNACK CUPS

Snack Cups are easy to make—and fun to make fancy with nuts and toppings and such.

What you need

1 package (3 oz.) Jell-O Gelatin, any flavor
1 cup boiling water
1 cup cold water
  Small paper cups
  Toppings—prepared whipped topping,
    sundae sauce, flaked coconut,
    chopped nuts, chopped or sliced fruit,
    marshmallow sauce, miniature
    marshmallows, colored sprinkles

What you do

1. Dissolve gelatin in boiling water in a medium bowl. Stir until all the gelatin is dissolved. Then add cold water and stir.

2. Pour gelatin into a pitcher that has a good pouring spout. Line up your paper cups on a tray. Carefully pour gelatin into the cups, just as you would pour orange juice.

3. Carefully place tray in refrigerator and chill until firm.

4. If you like your supersnack fancy, spoon on some prepared whipped topping or sundae sauce. Or sprinkle with coconut, nuts, fruit, or marshmallows.

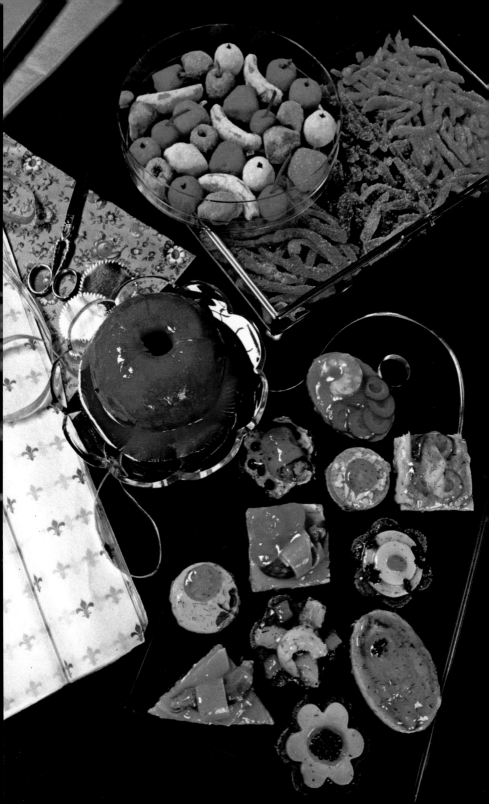

Things You Never Thought Of

Could you ever imagine Jell-O Gelatin becoming—

- crunchy candied orange peel
- marzipan fruits for holiday gifts
- a quick glaze for baked ham
- rosy cinnamon apples for a cozy dessert?

Enter the world of eating delights with these out-of-the-ordinary recipes. It's almost like magic, the way Jell-O Gelatin changes its form to become things you never thought of.

GLAZED HORS d'OEUVRES
(photographed on page 108)

1⅔ cups water
⅛ teaspoon whole black pepper
½ bay leaf
½ teaspoon dried dill
1 package (3 oz.) Jell-O Lemon Gelatin
½ teaspoon salt
Dash of cayenne
3 tablespoons vinegar
14 open-faced appetizer-size
sandwiches*

*Or 6 open-faced sandwiches

If gelatin glaze becomes too firm to pour, soften the glaze a few minutes over hot water.

Combine water, pepper, bay leaf, and dill; cover and simmer for about 10 minutes. Strain. Dissolve gelatin and salt in the hot liquid. Add cayenne and vinegar. Chill until syrupy.

Place sandwiches on a rack. Pour a thin layer of the syrupy gelatin over each. Chill until set but not firm; then pour a second layer of gelatin over each. Chill until firm—about 1 hour. Makes about 1¾ cups glaze.

Sandwich suggestions:

Buttered rye bread topped with tomato slices and sliced cooked ham rolled around asparagus spears. Garnish with chopped ripe olives.

Salty rye bread spread with horseradish and chili sauce and topped with tiny shrimp.

Pumpernickel bread spread with cream cheese and topped with smoked salmon.

Buttered whole wheat bread topped with cranberry sauce or cranberry-orange relish and sliced turkey. Garnish with whole walnuts and thin orange slices.

Pumpernickel bread spread with mustard and topped with Swiss cheese, sauerkraut, and corned beef. Garnish with dill pickle slices.

Buttered rye bread spread with horseradish and topped with sliced roast beef and wedges of tomato.

PASTEL CANDIED FRUIT PEEL
(photographed on page 108)

> 3 large grapefruit (free from blemishes)*
> 2 packages (3 oz. each) or 1 package (6 oz.) Jell-O Gelatin, any fruit flavor
> 2 cups water
> 2 cups sugar
> 1 large stick cinnamon
> ½ teaspoon whole cloves

*Or use 6 large oranges.

Cut grapefruit in halves; squeeze juice. Cover squeezed grapefruit halves with water in a saucepan. Bring to a boil; boil 15 minutes. Drain. Remove pulp from peel and with bowl of spoon carefully remove moist white membrane. Cut peel into thin strips, about ¼ inch wide. Return to saucepan; cover with water and boil again for 15 minutes, or until easily pierced with a fork. Drain. Mix gelatin, 2 cups water, and 1 cup of the sugar in a heavy skillet. Add prepared peels and spices. Bring to a boil; reduce heat to medium and continue cooking, stirring occasionally, until peels are translucent and syrup is almost absorbed—about 50 minutes. Remove from heat.

If desired, parboiled peels may be cut in fancy shapes using hors d'oeuvre cutters or a pointed sharp knife to make attractive food decorations.

Lift peels, a few at a time, from skillet with a fork. Toss peels in remaining 1 cup sugar. Arrange in a single layer on wax paper-lined trays; let dry about 12 hours or overnight. Store in a tightly covered container. Makes about 1 pound.

MARZIPAN
(photographed on page 108)

1¾ cups (about) Baker's Cookie Coconut
1 package (3 oz.) Jell-O Gelatin,
  any flavor
1 cup ground blanched almonds
⅔ cup sweetened condensed milk
1½ teaspoons sugar
1 teaspoon almond extract

Combine all ingredients and mix until well blended. Shape into small fruits or vegetables by hand, or use small candy molds. If desired, use food coloring to paint details on fruit; add whole cloves or citron or angelica for stems and blossom ends. Chill until dry; then store at room temperature in covered container. Makes about 3 cups or 36 confections.

Appropriate flavors for various fruits and vegetables are: strawberry flavor gelatin for strawberries; lemon flavor gelatin for grapefruit, bananas, lemon, Bartlett pears; Concord grape flavor gelatin for grapes; lime flavor gelatin for green apples, leaves, stems, limes; orange flavor gelatin for carrots, pumpkins, tangerines, oranges; cherry or black cherry flavor gelatin for cherries.

FRUITED GELATIN GLAZE
(for Cream Pie or Cheesecake)

1 package (3 oz.) Jell-O Strawberry or
  Raspberry Gelatin
1 cup boiling water
1 package (10 oz.) Birds Eye Quick Thaw
  Strawberries or Red Raspberries

Dissolve gelatin in boiling water. Add strawberries; stir until fruit is separated and mixture is thickened. Chill, if necessary. Spoon over top of chilled 9-inch cream pie, with fluted edge, or a 9- or 10-inch cheesecake. Makes about 2¼ cups glaze.

CINNAMON GLAZED APPLES
(photographed on page 108)

  2 packages (3 oz. each) or 1 package (6 oz.) Jell-O Strawberry-Banana Gelatin
  1 cup water
  1 cup apple juice
  1 cinnamon stick, about 2 inches long*
  3 lemon slices, ¼ inch thick
  6 medium baking apples, peeled and cored

*Or use ¼ teaspoon ground cinnamon.

Combine gelatin, water, apple juice, cinnamon stick, and lemon slices in medium skillet. Bring to a boil, stirring until gelatin is dissolved. Add apples; cover and simmer 15 minutes, or until almost tender, turning once and basting occasionally. Remove from heat. Cool apples in syrup; remove cinnamon stick and lemon slices. Place apples in 6 custard cups or serving dishes and top with syrup. Chill until set—about 1 hour. Serve with whipped topping, if desired. Makes 6 servings.

FIG-BERRY PRESERVES

  3 cups mashed figs (about 20 medium figs)*
  2 packages (3 oz. each) or 1 package (6 oz.) Jell-O Strawberry Gelatin
  3 cups (1¼ lb.) sugar

*If dark figs are used, preserves will be a deep purple color. For lighter preserves, figs may be peeled.

Thoroughly mix figs, gelatin, and sugar in a *large* saucepan. Bring to a boil over medium heat and continue boiling for 3 minutes, stirring occasionally. Pour quickly into glasses. Cover at once with ⅛ inch hot paraffin. Store in refrigerator. Makes 4⅓ cups or about 6 (6-fl. oz.) glasses.

CRANBERRY JELLY CANDY

- 1 can (16 oz.) jellied cranberry sauce
- 3 packages (3 oz. each) Jell-O Cherry, Raspberry, *or* Orange Gelatin
- 1 cup sugar
- ½ bottle Certo Fruit Pectin ·
- 1 cup chopped nuts
  Additional sugar or Baker's Angel Flake or Cookie Coconut

Beat cranberry sauce until smooth. Bring to a boil over high heat. Stir in gelatin and sugar; simmer 10 minutes, stirring frequently until dissolved. Remove from heat. Stir in fruit pectin; then add nuts and stir 10 minutes to prevent nuts from floating. Pour into buttered 9-inch square pan. Chill until firm—about 2 hours. Invert onto wax paper which has been sprinkled with additional sugar or coconut. Cut candy into ¾ inch squares with spatula that has been dipped in warm water; roll in sugar. After about an hour, roll in sugar again to prevent stickiness. Makes about 2 pounds candy.

Give candies for gifts—
with a professional touch.
Tuck individual candies
into bonbon cups or
the tiny foil cups used for
baking small cupcakes.

ORANGE-GLAZED HAM

- 2 pound canned ham
  Whole cloves
- 1 package (3 oz.) Jell-O Orange Gelatir
- ½ cup firmly packed brown sugar

Allow ham to stand in can at room temperature for 2 to 3 hours. Remove from can, reserving any excess gelatinous natural ham juices. Place ham in baking dish. Insert cloves in top of ham. Combine ¼ cup of the reserved ham juices with the gelatin and brown sugar; spoon over ham. Bake at 325° until thoroughly heated —about 30 minutes, basting frequently during baking. Remove ham to serving platter; stir remaining ham juices into drippings in pan. Heat and stir just until blended; serve as a sauce for the sliced ham. Makes 6 servings.

FRUIT FLAVOR MARSHMALLOWS

1 package (3 oz.) Jell-O Gelatin,
  any flavor
½ cup boiling water
¾ cup sugar
3 tablespoons light corn syrup
  Confectioners sugar

Dissolve gelatin in boiling water in a saucepan over very low heat. Add sugar; cook and stir just until sugar is dissolved. (Do not boil.) Blend in corn syrup. Chill until slightly thickened. Beat at highest speed of electric mixer until mixture is thickened and will stand in soft peaks—about 8 to 10 minutes. Pour into an 8-inch square pan which has been lined on sides and bottom with waxed paper and the paper greased with butter or margarine. Chill overnight.

Turn firm mixture out onto a board heavily dusted with confectioners sugar. Carefully peel off waxed paper and dust surfaces heavily with sugar. Cut into 1-inch squares or into shapes, using small cookie cutters dipped in sugar. Roll cut edges in sugar. Store tightly covered. Makes about 5 dozen confections.

Basic Preparation Hints

Jell-O Gelatin is many things to many people.
But whatever form it takes, there are many
tips and hints to help you make a Jell-O Gelatin
dish the best, the easiest, and the fastest
way possible.

This chapter is divided into three sections—
definitions, techniques, and tips. Find out
the "how to's" and the special techniques to
help you prepare the recipes in this book.
Learn what you can do with Jell-O Gelatin—
cube it, whip it, flake it, layer it. Find out
how to add fruits and vegetables, how to
double recipes, as well as turn it out in
glorious molds.

Begin with these basics. Turn the simple into
the exotic. Experience the wide and wonderful
world of Jell-O Gelatin.

I. DEFINITION OF PREPARATION TERMS

To help you understand the various thickened stages of Jell-O Gelatin as stated in the recipes in this book, the following terms may be used as your guidelines:

CHILL UNTIL SLIGHTLY THICKENED

Definition:
Consistency of unbeaten egg whites.

Usage:
When you fold a creamy mixture or ingredient into gelatin, such as cream cheese or whipped topping, and when gelatin is to be whipped with ice bath.

CHILL UNTIL THICKENED

Definition:
Spoon drawn through gelatin leaves a definite impression.

Usage:
When you add fruit, vegetables, or other solid ingredients to gelatin.

SET BUT NOT FIRM

Definition:
Gelatin sticks to finger when touched and mounds or moves to side when tilted.

Usage:
When you layer gelatin. This describes desired consistency of each layer of gelatin before addition of next layer.

FIRM

Definition:
Gelatin does not mound or move when mold is tilted and does not stick to finger.

Usage:
When gelatin is to be unmolded.

II. TECHNIQUES FOR PREPARING JELL-O GELATIN

HOW TO UNMOLD GELATIN

Allow gelatin to set until firm—several hours or overnight.

Use a small pointed knife, dipped in warm water, to loosen top edge. Or, moisten tips of fingers and gently pull gelatin from edge of mold.

Dip mold, just to the rim, in warm (not hot) water—about 10 seconds. Lift from water, hold upright, and shake slightly to loosen gelatin.

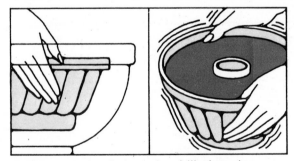

Moisten top of gelatin and a *chilled* serving plate with cold water. Moistened plate allows gelatin to be moved.

Place moistened plate over mold and invert.

Lift off mold carefully—if gelatin doesn't release easily, dip the mold in warm water again. If necessary, move gelatin to center of plate.

SPECIAL DECORATIVE MOLD OFFER

To create a fancy Jell-O Gelatin form, send for these molds. (LIMITED OFFER)

Large Ring Mold. For this 1½-quart copper-tone ring mold, send only $1.75 plus 6 Jell-O package fronts to: Ring Mold Special, Box 3034, Kankakee, Ill. 60901.

Individual Fluted Molds. To obtain 6 bright aluminum molds, send $1.00, 6 Jell-O package fronts, and your name and address to: Jell-O Molds, Box 3035, Kankakee, Ill. 60901.

Individual Ring Molds. For 6 copper-tone molds, send $1.50, 6 Jell-O package fronts, and your name and address to: Individual Ring Molds, Box 3036, Kankakee, Ill. 60901.

Tall Crown Mold. Or get a deep 2-quart copper-tone mold—send $2.00, 6 Jell-O package fronts, your name and address to: Tall Crown Mold, Box 3037, Kankakee, Ill. 60901.

RECOMMENDED SERVING SIZES OF JELL-O GELATIN MOLDS

Type of Mold	Average Serving
Clear desserts or salads	½ cup
Whipped desserts or salads	¾ cup
Relish salads	⅓ cup
Entree salads	about 1 cup
8-inch pie	6 servings
9-inch pie	7 servings

FLAVOR DUETS

- 2 packages (3 oz. each) Jell-O Gelatin (2 fruit flavors—see note)
- 2 cups boiling water
- 2 cups cold water

Dissolve gelatins together in boiling water. Add cold water. Pour into 1-quart bowl, individual molds, or dessert dishes. Chill until firm. Makes 4 cups, or 8 servings.

Note: Preferred flavor combinations include lemon with any red flavor, lemon with orange, raspberry with orange, lemon with orange-pineapple, and any two red flavors.

SPEED-SET JELL-O GELATIN

To use ice cubes, dissolve Jell-O Gelatin in boiling water as directed on package; then add 2 cups ice cubes for 3-oz. package or 4 cups ice cubes for 6-oz. package. Stir about 3 minutes to melt ice, or until gelatin is thickened. Remove any unmelted ice. Pour into serving dishes. Chill until soft set, about 30 minutes.

To use ice and water mixture, dissolve Jell-O Gelatin in boiling water as directed on package; then substitute a mixture of ice cubes or crushed ice and water for the cold water, stirring until ice melts completely. Chill.

To add fruits or vegetables or to whip, let gelatin stand 5 or 6 minutes to thicken after removing unmelted ice. Then fold in ingredients or whip. Chill until firm.

To use premeasured frozen mold, freeze ¾ cup water in a 2- or 3-cup mold for 3-oz. package or 1½ cups water in a 1-quart mold for 6-oz. package. Then dissolve gelatin in boiling water as directed on package and pour hot mixture over ice in mold. Stir until ice is dissolved, or until gelatin starts to thicken. If ice does not melt completely, remove unmelted pieces before chilling mold. To add fruits or vegetables, freeze water in a larger mold to allow space for adding ingredients and allow gelatin to stand 3 to 4 minutes to thicken before folding in the ingredients. Chill until firm.

HOW TO FLAKE JELL-O GELATIN

   1 package (3 oz.) Jell-O Gelatin
        (any fruit flavor)
   1 cup boiling water
   ¾ cup cold water

Dissolve gelatin in boiling water. Add cold water. Pour into a shallow pan. Chill until firm— at least 4 hours. Break into small flakes with a fork or force through a ricer or large-meshed strainer. Pile lightly in dishes. Top with fruit or ice cream, if desired. Makes 1 ¾ cups, or 4 servings.

HOW TO CUBE JELL-O GELATIN

1 package (3 oz.) Jell-O Gelatin
(any fruit flavor)
1 cup boiling water
¾ cup cold water*

*For very firm cubes, cold water may be reduced to ½ cup. For softer cubes, cold water may be increased to 1 cup.

Dissolve gelatin in boiling water. Add cold water. Pour into a shallow pan. Chill until firm—at least 4 hours or overnight. (Cubes hold their shape best when gelatin is chilled overnight.) Then cut in cubes, using sharp knife which has been dipped in hot water. To remove cubes from pan, apply warm wet cloth over bottom of pan; then remove with spatula. Or quickly dip pan in warm water and invert on wax paper. Serve in sherbet glasses with cream or fruit, if desired. Makes 4 servings.

HOW TO WHIP JELL-O GELATIN

Prepare Jell-O Gelatin (any fruit flavor) as directed on package and chill until very thick. Then beat with rotary beater or electric mixer until mixture is fluffy and thick—about double in volume results in the best eating quality and flavor.

To shorten the chilling and beating times, chill the gelatin until slightly thickened. Then place the bowl of gelatin in another bowl of ice and water before starting to beat.

Pour whipped gelatin into molds or shallow pan, or add cubes of Jell-O Gelatin or fruit and pour into molds. Chill until firm. Unmold, cut in squares, or spoon into serving dishes; serve with fruit or a custard sauce, if desired. A 3-oz. package makes about 4 cups, or 4 or 5 servings; a 6-oz. package makes about 8 cups, or 8 to 10 servings.

III. TIPS ON PREPARING JELL-O GELATIN

To prepare Jell-O Gelatin, dissolve the gelatin completely in boiling water or other liquid—for a clear, uniformly set mold, gelatin *must* be completely dissolved. Then add cold liquid.

To double a recipe, use two 3-oz. packages or one 6-oz. package of Jell-O Gelatin and twice the amounts of the other ingredients except salt, vinegar, and lemon juice—you'll find about 1½ times the amounts of these ingredients are sufficient.

For large molds, decrease the required liquid about ¼ cup for each 3 ounces of Jell-O Gelatin. (This has already been done in many recipes in this book for your convenience.)

For soft-set Jell-O Gelatin, increase liquid about ½ cup for each 3 ounces of Jell-O Gelatin—this is too soft to unmold, but has excellent eating quality.

To add fruits and vegetables, chill the gelatin until thickened, not set, before adding other ingredients. If gelatin isn't thick enough, fruits and vegetables may float or sink. (Do *not* add fresh or frozen pineapple, figs, mangoes, or papayas or frozen fruit juice blends containing these fruits—an enzyme in these fruits, when fresh, keeps Jell-O Gelatin from setting. When cooked or canned, these fruits are excellent in Jell-O Gelatin.)

To mold Jell-O Gelatin, pour it into molds or serving dishes—a 3-oz. package without fruits or vegetables makes 2 cups, a 6-oz. package makes 4 cups. Chill until firm.
(Any metal pan, bowl, cup, or can may be used as a mold.)

To layer gelatin mixtures, chill each layer until set, but not firm, before adding the next layer—if the first layer is too firm, the layers may slip apart when unmolded. Many layers may be built up in this way. Except for the first layer, the gelatin mixtures should be cool and slightly thickened before being poured into mold—if mixture is warm, it may soften the layer beneath and mixtures may run or mix together.

To make special designs, foods can be arranged in gelatin to make a simple mold more decorative in two ways:

Simple way: Chill gelatin until thick; then pour about ¼ inch gelatin into mold. Place a design of fruits or vegetables in gelatin. Chill until set, but not firm. Then pour remaining cooled gelatin into mold.

Expert way: Pour about ⅛ inch of gelatin into mold; chill until set, but not firm. Cool remaining gelatin. Arrange design on set gelatin, cover carefully with a few spoonfuls cooled gelatin to anchor design, and chill until set, but not firm. Then pour remaining cooled gelatin into the mold.

To chill gelatin molds, leave mold in refrigerator until firm.

Since metal chills more quickly than glass, gelatin in metal molds will be firm in less time than gelatin in a glass mixing bowl or serving dish.

To hasten chilling, chill the mold a few minutes in a pan of ice and water before placing in refrigerator.

For storage overnight or longer, it's wise to cover the gelatin to prevent evaporation and drying.

To make one serving, dissolve 1 ¾ tablespoons Jell-O Gelatin in ½ cup boiling water. Chill until firm.

Serve it in Style

Now that you've selected your own list of recipes-to-try-first, consider the varied and interesting containers and serving pieces you can use. Pull down those wedding gift wine goblets from the top shelf and look through the china cupboard for small soufflé dishes or custard cups. Think of the everyday as well as the unusual for your containers. With the shimmering colors of Jell-O Gelatin, you can easily achieve stunning settings for desserts and salads. Just use your imagination and what you have on hand.

Crystal and glass

custard cups
sherbet glasses
salad bowls
wine glasses, and other stemware
parfait and sundae glasses
pilsener glasses, small mugs
punch cups and small punch bowls
whiskey sour glasses, small brandy snifters
salad or canape plates
nappies or small dessert dishes
old cut-glass cake plates,
    compotes, sauce dishes, dinner plates
large glass bowls

China

large and individual soufflé dishes
rice bowls
bouillon cups
coffee and tea cups
pots de crème cups

Clear plastic

salad bowls and servers
wine and champagne glasses
individual dessert glasses

Index

Alaska Surprise, 60
Antipasto Salad, 68
Appetizers
    glazed hors d'oeuvres, 110
Artichoke Salad, 96

Banana-Marshmallow Special, 103
Banana Nut Ring with Ginger
    Topping, 54
Barbecue Salad, 79
Black Raspberry Ice Cream Dessert, 15
Brandied Cherry Ring, 58

Cakes
    crown jewel cake, 50
Candies
    cranberry jelly candy, 114
    fruit flavor marshmallows, 115
    marzipan, 112
    pastel candied fruit peel, 111
Carrot, Celery, and Olive Salad, 83
Cherry Burgundy Dessert, 35
Cherry Chiffon, 39
Chicken Mousse, 74
Chiffon Marble, 16
Cinnamon Glazed Apples, 113
Coffee Cream Dessert, 62
Cool Coleslaw Salad, 83
Cool Cubes, 102
Cranberry Jelly Candy, 114
Creamy Bleu Cheese Salad, 95
Crown Jewel Cake, 50
Cubed Gelatin, 12
Cucumber-Sour Cream Mold, 82

Definitions
    preparation terms, 117

Desserts
    alaska surprise, 60
    banana-marshmallow special, 103
    banana nut ring with ginger
        topping, 54
    black raspberry ice cream dessert, 15
    brandied cherry ring, 58
    cherry burgundy dessert, 35
    cherry chiffon, 39
    chiffon marble, 16
    cinnamon glazed apples, 113
    coffee cream dessert, 62
    cool cubes, 102
    crown jewel cake, 50
    cubed gelatin, 12
    double orange whip, 26
    double strawberry dessert, 13
    dream parfait, 102
    easy fruit tarts, 46
    fresh strawberry pie, 31
    frosted fresh grapes, 14
    frosty mandarin dessert, 29
    fruit delight, 22
    fruit flavor flakes, 27

FRONT COVER DESSERTS
Melon Bubble, 37
Chiffon Marble, 16
Gelatin mold with fruit
    (See Tips for Jell-O, 122)

BACK COVER DESSERTS
Ported Cherry Dessert, 36
Crown Jewel Cake, 50
Under-The-Sea Pear Salad, 69

fruit refresher, 23
gelatin and fruit, 12
ginger peach dessert, 23
grasshopper dessert, 52
honey pecan bavarian, 51
jellied ginger-upper, 14
jellied holiday nog, 42
jellied peach melba, 28
jellied prune whip, 30
jiffy cooler, 103
key lime pie, 48
kicky cooler, 102
layered bavarian, 27
layered parfait mold, 47
lemon chiffon pie, 38
mardi gras mold, 51
melon bubble, 37
melon cooler, 10
orange chiffon pie, 38
orange parfait, 26
orange-pineapple bavarian, 63
orange snow, 15
parfait pie, 59
pastel dessert, 30
patriotic mold, 61
peach-banana dessert, 22
peach bavarian, 11
peach gem pie, 53
pink lady pie, 43
pop art parfaits, 102
ported cherry dessert, 36
quick crème de menthe frappe, 18
quick fruit dessert, 10
rainbow parfait, 102
richelieu mold, 58
ring around the fruit mold, 62
snack cups, 102
strawberries romanoff, 34
strawberry bavarian pie, 59
strawberry supreme, 49
strawberry yogurt whip, 17
supersodas, 106
topaz parfait, 35
wine gelatin dessert, 18
winter fruit mold, 55
Double Orange Whip, 26
Double Strawberry Dessert, 13
Dream Parfait, 102

Easy Fruit Tarts, 46
Entrees
chicken mousse, 74
Florida seacoast salad, 75
green goddess salad bowl, 66
jellied salad nicoise, 67
jellied turkey platter, 87
keep fit luncheon platter, 86
orange-glazed ham, 114
quick chicken cranberry mold
platter, 91
Spanish tuna salad luncheon
platter, 90

Entrees (continued)
turkey-soufflé salad, 71

Fig-Berry Preserves, 113
Florida Seacoast Salad, 75
Fresh Fruit Salad, 94
Fresh Strawberry Pie, 31
Frosted Fresh Grapes, 14
Frosty Mandarin Dessert, 29
Fruit Delight, 22
Fruited Gelatin Glaze, 112
Fruit Flavor Flakes, 27
Fruit Flavor Marshmallows, 115
Fruit Refresher, 23

Garden Soufflé Salad, 70
Gelatin and Fruit, 12
Ginger Peach Dessert, 23
Glazed hors d'oeuvres, 110
Grasshopper Dessert, 52
Green Goddess Salad Bowl, 66

Honey Pecan Bavarian, 51

Ingredients for Jell-O, 6, 7

Jellied Avocado Ring, 98
Jellied Fresh Vegetable Salad, 81
Jellied Gazpacho, 78
Jellied Ginger-Upper, 14
Jellied Holiday Nog, 42
Jellied Salad Nicoise, 67
Jellied Peach Melba, 28
Jellied Prune Whip, 30
Jellied Turkey Salad, 87
Jellied Waldorf Salad, 82
Jiffy Cooler, 103

Key Lime Pie, 48
Kicky Cooler, 102

Layered Bavarian, 27
Layered Cranberry-Apple Mold, 98
Layered Parfait Mold, 47
Lemon Chiffon Pie, 38

Mardi Gras Mold, 51
Marzipan, 112
Melon Bubble, 37
Melon Cooler, 10
Minted Pineapple Relish, 11
Miscellaneous
fig-berry preserves, 113
fruited gelatin glaze, 112
Mold Offer, 119
Molded Ham and Egg Salad, 86
Molded Potato Salad, 97
Molded Tomato Relish, 19
Molded Vegetable Relish, 99

Orange Chiffon Pie, 38
Orange-Glazed Ham, 114

Orange Parfait, 26
Orange-Pineapple Bavarian, 63
Orange Snow, 15

Parfaits
  cool cubes, 102
  dream parfait, 102
  kicky cooler, 102
  layered parfait mold, 47
  orange parfait, 26
  parfait pie, 59
  pop art parfaits, 102
  rainbow parfait, 102
  topaz parfait, 35
Parfait Pie, 59
Patriotic Mold, 61
Pastel Candied Fruit Peel, 111
Pastel Dessert, 30
Peach-Banana Dessert, 22
Peach Bavarian, 11
Peach Gem Pie, 53
Pies
  fresh strawberry pie, 31
  key lime pie, 48
  lemon chiffon pie, 38
  orange chiffon pie, 38
  parfait pie, 59
  peach gem pie, 53
  pink lady pie, 43
  strawberry bavarian pie, 59
Pink Lady Pie, 43
Pop Art Parfaits, 102
Ported Cherry Dessert, 36

Quick Cranberry-Apple Mold, 91
Quick Crème de Menthe Frappé, 18
Quick Fruit Dessert, 10
Quick Orange Salad, 19

Rainbow Parfait, 102
Relishes
  minted pineapple relish, 11
  molded tomato relish, 19
  molded vegetable relish, 99
Richelieu Mold, 58
Ring Around The Fruit Mold, 62

Salads
  antipasto salad, 68
  artichoke salad, 96
  barbecue salad, 79
  carrot, celery, and olive salad, 83
  chicken mousse, 74
  cool coleslaw salad, 83
  creamy bleu cheese salad, 95
  cucumber-sour cream mold, 82
  Florida seacoast salad, 75
  fresh fruit salad, 94
  garden soufflé salad, 70
  green goddess salad bowl, 66
  jellied avocado ring, 98
  jellied fresh vegetable salad, 81

jellied gazpacho, 78
jellied salad nicoise, 67
jellied turkey salad, 87
jellied waldorf salad, 82
layered cranberry-apple mold, 98
molded ham and egg salad, 86
molded potato salad, 97
molded vegetable relish, 99
quick cranberry-apple mold, 91
quick orange salad, 19
salmon dill mousse, 95
sequin salad, 97
snappy fruit mold, 79
Spanish tuna salad, 90
turkey-soufflé salad, 71
under-the-sea pear salad, 69
zesty ginger-fruit salad, 80
Salmon Dill Mousse, 95
Sequin Salad, 97
Snack Cups, 107
Snappy Fruit Mold, 79
Spanish Tuna Salad, 90
Strawberries Romanoff, 34
Strawberry Bavarian Pie, 59
Strawberry Chiffon, 39
Strawberry Supreme, 49
Strawberry Yogurt Whip, 17
Supersodas, 106

Techniques
  flavor duets, 47, 119
  how to cube Jell-O, 12, 50, 121
  how to flake Jell-O, 27, 120
  how to whip Jell-O, 15, 121
  serving sizes of molds, 42, 119
  speed set, 119-120
    ice cube method, 16, 120
    ice/water method, 18, 97, 120
    premeasured frozen mold, 120
    to add fruits/vegetables, 120
  to vary flavor, 26
  unmolding gelatin, 19, 28, 118
Tips
  chilling gelatin molds, 78, 123
  doubling recipes, 35, 122
  for soft set, 122
  large molds, 122
  layering, 55, 123
  special designs, 123
  to add carbonated beverages, 10
  to add fruits/
    vegetables, 11, 14, 22, 122
  to make one serving, 123
  to store overnight, 95, 123
Topaz Parfait, 35
Turkey-Soufflé Salad, 71

Under-The-Sea Pear Salad, 69

Wine Gelatin Dessert, 18
Winter Fruit Mold, 55

Zesty Ginger-Fruit Salad, 80